Scotland's Aviation History

Arthur W. J. G. Ord - Hume

The BAC 1-11 was the mainstay of the short-haul airlines for almost a quarter of a century and British Caledonian operated a large number of these in the 1970s and 1980s on the London–Glasgow route. Both G-ASJE and G-ASJH joined the fleet on November 1st, 1971 and, eleven years later, they were sold to America. This picture was taken shortly after their arrival at London's Gatwick Airport and looks east to the Southern Region railway visible on the embankment in the background.

Stenlake Publishing Ltd

First Published in the United Kingdom, 2014
Stenlake Publishing Limited
54-58 Mill Square, Catrine, KA5 6RD
01290 551122
www.stenlake.co.uk

Printed by
Blissetts,
Roslin Road
Acton, W3 8DH

ISBN 978-1-84033-653-5

Preface and Acknowledgements

I spent much of my early life in Scotland where the family home was between Leith and Portobello at a time when those places were quiet and traffic was minimal. It was also a stone's throw from where Tytler had landed after one of his pioneering, if largely uncontrolled, ascents in his 18th century 'Edinburgh Fire Balloon'. My grandfather was a composer and musician and the family had to divide time between the Lothians and the curious land to the south. This tended to give me an uncertain sense of identity for at school in Edinburgh I was 'that English boy' while down south I was 'that Scotch *[sic]* boy'. By the time I joined the Royal Air Force, though, there was no more personality division and, helpfully, my initial posting was to Leuchars where I was able to indulge in golf and flying in more or less equal quantities.

In those immediate post-war days as war conditions wound down to a morbid peacetime austerity, I suddenly discovered that most people, including, to my horror, too many fellow Scots, thought that aviation had all been a thing dreamed up south of the Border and that all Scotland had contributed to aviation was welcoming the first Englishman to land his aeroplane on Highland soil with a skirl o'the pipes and a wee dram. Nobody seemed to think that anything aeronautically significant had happened north of the Border! The Scots hadn't done anything to advance flying!

I knew that was wrong and that while injustice was one thing, *self-imposed* injustice was quite another, something ought to be done about it. So this book is the culmination of some 65 years of contemplation… It was, however, my publisher, Richard Stenlake, who during one of his visits to my present home in Southern England, suggested to me that I might be the one to put things a-right. This book, then, is partly his fault.

In offering this as the outcome, I have to express grateful thanks to others who have collaborated. Peter Lewis researched some of the Scottish pioneers for his Putnam book in 1962, work subsequently revised by friends Michael Goodall and the late Albert E Tagg for an American publisher in 2001. I acknowledge their assistance.

As for illustrations, first I must thank the late John Neilan, one-time Aberdeen Airways' pilot. Both of us worked on developing the Britten-Norman Islander on the Isle of Wight – an aircraft not unfamiliar to many Scots in remote places who depend on air services for their wherewithal. I now have John's personal photographic records in my collection and will be sharing some of them with you. Thanks to Stuart and Dougal McIntyre, grandson and son, respectively, of David McIntyre.

Three more good friends, two of whom I have known since I was a youthful bike-riding spotter and one whose father and I used to fly around the 1950s air-shows, have helped me add extra illustrations to my collection – George Cull, Mike Hooks and Richard Riding. And Richard Stenlake, more than mere publisher, has dived deeply into his valuable private collection of Scottish picture postcards to add to my own extensive collection of Scottish aviation material. My thanks to all these for their help.

G-AGZG was a Scottish Aviation Ltd DC-3 passenger conversion for its subsidiary, Scottish Airlines Ltd. It is pictured here at Renfrew in February 1947. Formerly WZ985, it gained its C of A on January 11th, 1946 and served the airline well until October 1952 when it went to the French air force as 42-23941. *Picture by E J Riding from the collection of Richard T Riding.*

Introduction

To present a comprehensive chronicle of the evolution of aviation in Scotland would be a tall order, in particular if the end result was to be a book that you and I could both afford and at the same time carry without risking personal physical injury. Consequently this small book is intended to offer an economic distillation of our aeronautical history, achievements and inventions in a form that shall be accurate, concise and, perforce, of use to you.

There is a popular myth, mostly put about by those who live south across the Border in the Peninsula, that nothing much aeronautical ever happened in Scotland. The Scots, they say, were introduced to artificial flight when Big Mechanical Birds driven by moustachioed men with Oxbridge accents and baggy trews arrived from conjoined England...

It's a nice story and one which perhaps we should continue to encourage while quietly smirking at the ignorance of the storyteller. There's only one problem and that is that it's a bit unfair and it's high time we told our side of the story!

The reality is that Scotland was easily level-pegging with the pioneers from elsewhere. We had our sights set on achievements in the air from earliest times. In fact we had flight, both real and mythical, at the same time as the English.

I mentioned the mythical side. This is not an indication of *negative* attainment, for mythical flight, in folklore, is just as important as the genuine flight that, sometime later, was to follow. Mythical flight reveals Man's imagination and what is Life if not built on creativity generated from imagination? As an example of the importance of myth, look across the Atlantic to the American Space programme. It all began as myth – the make-believe of the boys' comic papers – yet when it actually came to pass, the names chosen for rockets and space-ships were those that had echoed through the pages of children's pulp fiction for decades. No, Man dreams fantasy, but all too often he turns that fantasy into hard reality.

Captioned 'The First Aeroplane to be seen at Montrose', this dramatic picture of a Maurice Farman S.7 Longhorn (70 hp Renault engine) was captured by a local photographer on February 26th, 1913. It was coming in to land at the end of an epic journey that had begun at Farnborough on February 13th. Piloted by Captain George William Patrick Dawes (1880-1960), it was the first Royal Flying Corps aeroplane to reach the newly-created station at Montrose which would be home to Farnborough's No. 2 Squadron. Allocated the Service number '207', this aircraft was rebuilt at Montrose after its punishing journey and then went to Ireland for the 1913 Military Manoeuvres. The life of these fragile aircraft was frequently short and 207 was no exception: it suffered a forced landing at Ballyhornan on September 24th and was neither retrieved nor repatriated.

As for the men who believed they could simply fly by flapping their arms about, have you ever watched a hang-glider or a powered paraglider flying?

Back to Scotland's part in the development of aviation. The pioneers who experimented with aviation long before the Wright Brothers made a valid contribution to world aviation knowledge. The first balloon to carry a man in the UK rose not far from what (after 1901) would become known as Edinburgh's Royal Mile and the first man-carrying glider to leave the ground in the UK flew through the skies of Cardross. Later the first tailless aircraft danced with the clouds over Ayrshire.

Aside from the early birds who gained notoriety, fame and a place in history but little else that was tangible, we managed to create an important aircraft manufacturing industry that served the British Isles well through two world wars. As transatlantic flight became an essential supporting link during the Second World War, we created and operated the most important international airport for the arrival of supplies and munitions from North America.

Because you cannot have achievement without people, it is worth mentioning that internationally-famous long-distance flyer and record-breaker James Allan 'Jim' Mollison (1905-1959) was born in Glasgow. Moffat-born Hugh Dowding (1882-1974) was Air Chief Marshall Fighter Command and steered Britain through the Battle of Britain. These are just two examples of the very many notable Scots in the history of British aviation. Of the 32 Victoria Crosses awarded to members of Britain's fighting forces during the war, six went to Scottish airmen. As individuals, Scots have made a notable impact on events.

As for the hardware, the first British-operated airliners to start up scheduled air services after the war were mainly ex-military aircraft converted for passenger use in Scotland. And we also had one of the last thriving independent aircraft manufacturing industries in the whole of the British Isles to add to a more than adequate roll of pioneers, movers and shakers.

And, in those fragile years of tenuous peace that characterised the second half of the 20th century, Britain's defence of its skies was wholly dependent on surveillance missions operated and maintained from Scottish air bases.

Even as a mere introductory summary, the foregoing indicates a pretty fair litany of achievement.

THE BEGINNINGS: MYTH, LEGEND AND HOT-AIR BALLOONISTS

For our starting point, we need to journey back to the time of James IV and recount the tale of John Damian who was allegedly of Italian origin. His real name was Giovanni Damiano de Falucci and he appears first in the records of the Scottish exchequer in January 1501 where he is referred to as 'Master John the French Leech'. This term of anything but endearment seems to have been inspired by his previous activities in France where he pretended to be a doctor and earned the reputation of being 'a killer in surgery'. In Scotland he landed firmly on his feet and served as a sort of Jack o'All Trades at the court of King James who had accorded him the title of Abbot of Tongland, Galloway. It seems Damian was a dabbler in alchemy, medicine and flying, career aspects that led to his rapid social advancement by the king. He indulged extensively in thaumaturgy but his place in our history was earned by his alleged attempt to fly from Stirling Castle. Not merely content with achieving flight, he boasted of his intention to fly to France. Apparently by September 1507 his repeated failure to succeed in alchemy earned him an understandable degree of royal disapproval and so Damian was inspired to try to replenish his status by a demonstration of his aerial capabilities.

When the appointed day arrived, Damian donned a pair of wings made from chicken feathers and enthusiastically flung himself from the highest point of the Stewart king's abode. It is related that he made landfall on a conveniently-positioned dung-heap which only partially cushioned his fall.

While he failed to achieve flight he had received a practical demonstration of gravity which rewarded him with a broken thigh. This led him to suggest that success would have been possible had he chosen eagle's feather instead of those from some other and obviously less aerodynamic avian species.

This gallant if stupid antic is based on the contemporary writing of the poet William Dunbar (1459-1522) and a later reference by the writer John Lesley (*The History of Scotland: From the Death of King James I, in the Year 1436 to the Year 1561; Edinburgh, 1830,* p.76). While poets were often the recorders of mediaeval events and contemporary writers the news reporters of the time, neither source can be totally relied upon. The story of the Bird Man of Stirling, great though it is, is best treated *cum grano salis*! If Flodden marked the end of James IV, it also coincided with the disappearance of Damian from court. His legend, though, lives on although you will seek in vain for the *engrailed brassen-plate* to mark the event at Stirling's great pile.

We are on much firmer footing with Scotland's next aviator, James Tytler (1745-1804). Tytler was an Angus man (Forfarshire as it was then known), an apothecary, writer and the editor of both the second and third editions of the *Encyclopaedia Britannica* having taken over from its founding compiler, the youthful and unfortunately-named William Smellie. Aside from his profession, Tytler was not just Scotland's first aeronaut, but became the first person to fly in a hot-air balloon anywhere in the whole of the British Isles.

Back in those days, the business of ballooning was embraced by that ancient yet recurring name – aérostation. It was associated with the 'aether' into which one might enter via an aérostat. The first practical demonstration of this arcane cunning came in 1783 with news that the brothers Joseph-Michel and Jacques-Étienne Montgolfier had made their ground-breaking hot-air balloon ascent near Paris, an event quickly followed by the third Frenchman to fly in a balloon, Jean-François Pilâtre de Rozier.

Tytler had opened a pharmacy in Leith near Edinburgh but this was not a financial success. Probably this was due to its owner's predilection for alcohol and he had to flee to England to escape his creditors. Returning to Edinburgh a few years later, he had amassed sufficient money to indulge in making what he described as his *Grand Edinburgh Fire Balloon*. Edinburgh's Comely Gardens had long fallen from favour. Said once to rival London's Vauxhall Gardens, the venue was rundown and consequently the proprietor Alexander Williamson jumped at the chance of attracting more spectators when Tytler proposed making use of the wall and tree-sheltered park for his trials.

Here Tytler experimented before a paying public (6d a time) to see his 13-foot diameter test balloon rise and fall, tethered by a length of string. On 28th June 1784 he had his full-size balloon ready.

Almost a month before the famed Italian Vincenzo Lunardi made the first of his many flights in London, Tytler became airborne on August 25th, 1784 in his balloon which was anything but balloon-like in

James Tytler (1775-1804) was the first person in the British Isles to ascend in a hot-air balloon in 1784. Born in Fearn, Angus, the son of a Presbyterian minister, he practised medicine and had a pharmacy in Leith for a while but had to flee to England to escape his creditors. However, he returned and triumphed over adversity to build and fly his 'Edinburgh Fire Balloon'. His pioneering activities were overshadowed by the subsequent flights of Lunardi. His biographers said of him that he 'did much hack work for low pay and rarely if ever emerged from poverty… a man of many talents - as a political and religious controversialist, scholar, journalist, poet, song writer, musician, balloonist, pharmacist, surgeon and printer.' However, while aviation seems to have forgotten him, his revision of the *Encyclopaedia Britannica* has ensured his place in the hall of fame.

The first balloon ascent anywhere in the British Isles took place in Edinburgh on August 25th, 1784, when James Tytler rose from the ground in his celebrated Edinburgh Fire Balloon. The balloon, hardly the elegant sphere of a Montgolfier or a Lunardi, carried with it a large stove to provide the hot air for lift. Hardly a pretty vehicle but a 'first' nevertheless. Here we see an admission ticket to view the balloon close-up for a staggering 3/-. Clearly Tytler, ever short of money and strong on debtors, did his best to make money where he could. He still died a forgotten pioneer, in a foreign land, and in debt. *Image from the Banks Collection, British Museum, with grateful thanks.*

appearance. His barrel-shaped envelope stood 40 feet high and had a diameter of 30 feet and was kept buoyant by the expedient of carrying its own heater – a 3-feet diameter stove! He only attained an altitude of a few feet but it was a great achievement and when, two days later, he tried again, he rose to a height of 350 feet and travelled the best part of half a mile to alight at Restalrig. He charged the public 'admission' to watch his attempts, the price of a ticket being an astonishing 3/-. On the 31st he made a second and longer flight. These would prove to be his best flights and subsequent attempts were less successful.

His last flight was on July 26th, 1785. It proved to be a disaster as a thunderstorm broke a few minutes after the process of inflation had begun. As the winds increased, the balloon was wrenched from the hands of his helpers and dashed to the ground, damaging the envelope and breaking the stove. With no money for repairs, this was the end of Tytler's gallant endeavours. Sadly both his public and the Edinburgh press turned against him reviling and ridiculing the man for his failures while ignoring his undisputed achievement. By then Lunardi had come to Scotland and proceeded to undertake five spectacular ascents to vast public acclaim. The incompetent former chemist from Leith was quickly forgotten. Once more in debt and bankrupt, he went to Ireland (leaving behind a tangle of women, only one of which was Mrs Tytler, and a lot of children) and from there eventually fled to America where in 1804, following a bout of earnest drinking, he was found drowned.

By this time Lunardi had made it to Edinburgh. Here the dashing Italian stole everybody's hearts. Back in London, a fashion fad had blossomed as ladies' skirts were decorated with balloon motifs. In Scotland the crazy fashion of the Lunardi Bonnet – a hat that stood two feet tall – was allegedly inspired by the man who was officially secretary to the Neapolitan ambassador. This impossible piece of head-gear was immortalised in the Robert Burns' poem *To a Louse,* penned about a lassie called Jenny who had one of these little pests scampering around inside her bonnet.

Lunardi flew a hydrogen-filled balloon from the grounds of George Heriot's School in Edinburgh in October 1785. He traversed the Firth of Forth to make landfall at Ceres near Cupar in Fife some 46 miles away. The balloon was later exhibited, inflated and airborne, inside St Mungo's Cathedral, Glasgow, where wide-eyed wonderers could view it for the expenditure of the arbitrary shilling. After a series of other grand flights in Scotland (including one involving a sound ducking in the North Sea for its illustrious pilot, and another in Newcastle where an unfortunate bystander was dragged into the air and fell to his death), the Italian left the British Isles rather hastily to fly his craft elsewhere in Europe.

His success had completely overshadowed the achievements of the less-fortunate Tytler who would remain largely forgotten until recent times. Even if habitually intoxicated and ever-short of the wherewithal to settle his accounts, to be trounced by an Italian was humiliation in the extreme. No wonder, then, that the

Angus man took his debts elsewhere and lost so much interest that he allowed himself to die.

Viewed in today's light, perhaps Tytler's flight was but a mere trifle – but it was the first in Britain. He was a victim of his own curious lifestyle aided and abetted by the fickleness of the ordinary public. Of the few accounts of his life and achievements, only that of Sir James Fergusson is of worth.

HEAVIER-THAN-AIR FLYING – THE PIONEERS

Aside from the ballonauts, Scotland's earliest heavier-than-air flyer was Percy Sinclair Pilcher (1866-1899) who flew his Lilienthal-type glider from Wallacetown Farm near Cardross in Dunbartonshire 110 years later in 1895. He later moved to Auchensail where, having rented a farmhouse with an accompanying large barn, he built a larger glider called *The Beetle*. His goal was to fit an engine to one of his gliders to convert to powered flight, a target which he closely approached.

Pilcher was born in Bath and following time in the Royal Navy he became an apprentice with a firm of Glasgow shipbuilders. In 1891 he took a job as assistant lecturer at Glasgow University where interest in aviation became a consuming interest. The outcome was a hang glider which he flew for the first time in 1895. He called it *The Bat*. By far and away the leading exponents of flight in Europe were the German Lilienthal brothers Otto (1848-1896) and Gustav (1849-1933). Pilcher, who fortuitously could speak German, sought out Otto and they discussed the precious little knowledge there was about gliding at the time. They shared their own experiences. Following this, Pilcher built two more gliders which he named *The Beetle* and *The Gull*. Leaning heavily on Lilienthal's work he then built a glider called *The Hawk* with which, in 1897, he broke the world distance record by flying 820 feet within the grounds of Stanford Hall near Lutterworth, Leicestershire.

Now with the goal of powered flight in his sights, he designed and began building a triplane to be fitted with a four-horsepower motor. The project pushed him into debt and it wasn't until September 1888 that it was completed. He planned a flight to demonstrate it before a group of onlookers and potential sponsors in a field near Stanford Hall. However, shortly before the day of the demonstration – the 30th – the engine broke its crankshaft. In order not to disappoint the crowd, Pilcher decided to fly the *Hawk* glider instead. The weather was bad with a fitful wind and driving rain but at four in the afternoon the conditions improved and Pilcher prepared to fly. A gust caught his glider snapping off the tail and the glider fell 30 feet to the ground. Poor Pilcher, seemingly so close to stealing a world lead on powered flight, died from his injuries two days later and the triplane never flew – publicly at least.

A full-sized replica of the *Hawk* glider is displayed in the National Museum of Scotland in Edinburgh while there is a replica of *The Bat* in Glasgow's Riverside Museum.

John William Dunne was a Boer War veteran and the son of a noted military general. Wounded in combat he was invalided back to Britain where he took up the study of aerodynamics while he regained health. His companion at this time was the author and visionary H G Wells who encouraged him to work with aircraft. Colonel Capper of Farnborough's Balloon Factory made him chief designer of military kites. Dunne dreamed of designing a completely stable aircraft but he got little encouragement from his workplace. Capper believed in him and fostered his design. All his development work up to making a powered version of his tailless biplane design was undertaken at Blair Atholl. Dunne's farsighted designs were so greatly removed from contemporary thinking that he was snubbed in Britain and had to see his ideas championed the other side of the Atlantic. Dunne died in 1949 in his 74th year. This portrait dates from 1912.

A remarkable innovator was John William Dunne (1875-1949). Dunne was actually born in Co Kildare but came to Scotland where he devised and developed a remarkable series of swept-wing tailless biplane gliders which he flew at Blair Atholl and Glen Tilt in the north of Perthshire. In truth, Dunne should have beaten the Americans into the world of heavier-than-air powered flight for his inspiration went back to the Boer War. He saw the advantages of airborne reconnaissance before there were aircraft! In a world where balloons were revered as high-tech eyes in the sky, Dunne's cries for something that didn't have to go with the wind fell on stopped-up ears. Four years would pass after he was invalided out of the Imperial Yeomanry with great ideas until at last somebody listened. Yet by 1904 he had virtually solved all the stability and control problems that his tailless aircraft would face. There were many models built and tested until he was ready for the real thing. He named his design after the gliding seeds of the cucumber plant – *zanonia*.

At last, through the aegis of his father, a recently-retired senior army general, somebody listened and trials were authorised to proceed. These tests were carried out in great secrecy between 1906 and 1909. The main trials took place from July 1907 on the estate of the Duke of Atholl (Lord John Murray of Tullibardine and Earl Strange) under the auspices of the War Office. So stringent was the security at the time that, even though there was enormous press interest, nobody got through the gillies that acted as guards against intruders and no reporter or camera lens got anywhere near the curious tailless biplane gliders that were flown there.

Conducted under Government supervision, these mysterious trials had begun at the Army Balloon Factory, Farnborough, in 1905 where Dunne developed his theories of tailless aeronautics. He sought the assistance of the unit's commanding officer, Colonel John Edward Capper, who quickly provided the necessary facilities and encouragement for the project which would be the first British military flying machine. After many trials and the building and testing of models, Dunne built a passenger-carrying glider which he called the D1. Construction took place in great secrecy and, in July of 1907, it was transported by train to the village of Blair Atholl for flight testing on Lord Tullibardine's estate.

It is hard to realise that this aircraft design actually made its first flight in 1907. Technically and aerodynamically, the Dunne biplane was years ahead of its time. Many of the early trials were carried out at Blair Atholl following some initial War Office interest and the assistance of the Balloon Factory at Farnborough, Hampshire. Four years of trials at the isolated site in Perthshire had established that Dunne's design was practical. The War Office, though, lost interest and decided it had no faith in heavier-than-air flight. Dunne went south again and, after enlisting the help of both Short Brothers (who helped build several of his designs) and Fairey, he ended up at Eastchurch and finally undertook further Army trials at Larkhill in 1914. An uninterested military rejected him and his design. Dunne gave up all aviation work immediately. What a loss to aviation! This picture from *The Illustrated London News* of August 23rd, 1913, shows his 8bis. biplane powered by an 80 hp Gnome rotary pusher engine.

With Colonel Capper as passenger, the arrow-shaped machine completed an eight-second flight from the duke's estate in the hills north of the village by Glen Tilt at the extreme north of Perthshire. Unfortunately the flight terminated in a crash in which passenger Capper was slightly injured, but the glider had succeeded in vindicating its designer's perseverance with what was, after all, a fairly outrageous design for its time.

Further trials continued during 1907 and 1908 which were supported by the British Army Council. There was a number of different aircraft ranging from the D.1-A and a powered version known as the D.1-B (which crashed on its first flight) to the D.2 training glider, designed but remaining unbuilt in 1907. The later Dunne-Huntington powered triplane, designed in 1907–1908, was flown successfully in 1911 as was the D.3 man-carrying glider back in 1908 and, in the same year, the D.4 powered airplane. This last had limited success and its designer described it as 'more a hopper than a flyer'.

In the interim, though, there had been something of a sea change at Farnborough and in 1909 the War Office ceased offering any official support for heavier-than-air flight. This was the time when advocates for anything other than balloons were greatly outnumbered by elderly but influential buffoons for whom war was inseparable from the horse, the balloon and the muzzle-loader. Enterprise and invention would be stifled for some while to come. Not surprisingly, under such circumstances, Dunne left the Balloon Factory and, having rustled up some financial investment from his friends and associates, set up a small company, the Blair Atholl Aeroplane Syndicate Ltd, to enable his experiments to continue.

His D.5 completed in 1910 proved to be a vast improvement over the previous designs. As with earlier models, the D.5 was a tailless biplane, with sharply swept-back wings. A central fuselage nacelle housed the pilot (and passenger) along with a rear-mounted engine which drove two pusher propellers. The swept wings provided inherent stability and incorporated wash-out by progressively decreasing the angle of incidence from root to tip. This marked the end of the Blair Atholl experiments and the whole operation was moved south to the Isle of Sheppey where the D.5 was demonstrated before no less than Orville Wright as well as the English ballooning ground-breaker and visionary Griffith Brewer (1867-1948).

Dunne's aircraft was inherently stable and could be flown hands-off using just the throttle to initiate a climb or descent. Although later he took his ideas to an enthusiastic America and while he subsequently went on to assist Geoffrey Hill in the design of Westland's own tailless aircraft, the Pterodactyl, Dunne's revolutionary tailless format for an aeroplane was eventually abandoned in favour of the so-called 'conventional' form. To this day it is understood that the tailless aircraft having swept-back wings incorporating wash-out at the tips creates a stable aerodyne. The first to establish this and support it with accurate aerodynamic formula was Dunne in Scotland.

In Dundee, another unsung pioneer of the unusual was Preston Watson. Preston Albert Watson (1881-1915) built four aircraft between 1903 and 1913. The first was a Wright-type glider but it was unsuccessful and scrapped. Years later members of his family claimed, without evidence, that it had indeed flown, an event which, if substantiated, would have made it one of the first flights in Britain.

Watson's next machine was his Biplane No.1, built to exploit his theory of aerodynamic stability by pivoting the top wing so that it could be rocked from side to side using a hanging control column. First flown as a glider, he subsequently fitted a 17-20 hp Dutheil et Chalmers twin-cylinder horizontally-opposed engine. In 1910, it was reconstructed as a glider for Dundee Aero Club.

Watson's Biplane No.2 was an improved version of the former and fitted with a four-wheeled undercarriage. It flew at Errol, Perthshire, during 1912. The Biplane No.2 that followed was powered by a six cylinder 45 hp Anzani. In 1914, Watson took his machine to Buc in France to compete in the Concours de la Securité en Aeroplane. Here it was flown but excluded because the pilot, one Samuel Summerfield, was declared 'a novice'.

That more or less ended Watson's aeronautical experiments and, with the outbreak of war, he joined the Royal Naval Air Service as a flight sub-lieutenant. Here he sustained injuries in action, was invalided back to Britain and died on June 30th 1915 in a military hospital at Uckfield, Sussex.

Preston Albert Watson lived and worked in Dundee where he hoped to become one of Scotland's aviation pioneers. In 1903 at the age of 22 he had built a Wright-type glider to which he later fitted a small French motor. Although his family later claimed that it had flown (which would have earned him the credit for being one of the earliest Britons – if not the first – to fly), this is both unproven and, sadly, unlikely. Between 1908 and 1909, he built a second machine known as the Biplane No.1. It was made of steel tube and bamboo and incorporated a then-novel rocking-wing system to provide roll and yaw control. This idea would be tried again in the 1930s in the Grice tandem-winged aircraft. Watson's machine was powered by a small French twin-cylinder engine, possibly the same as used in the earlier example. Pictured here in a rather industrial setting with its creator, it did not fly and was later rebuilt as a glider used by the Dundee Aero Club in 1910. Watson persevered building two more machines on the same principle. These did, apparently, fly, but the pivoted wing was of dubious merit. The outbreak of the First World War put an end to Watson's experiments. As a flight-sub-lieutenant in the Royal Naval Air Service he was gravely injured and repatriated to die in a Sussex military hospital in 1915.

Watson's pivoting wing was adopted by other inventors, specifically, Joseph Brindley Gurney Grice (1898-1983) and his curious Mosquito light aeroplane of 1935. That, also, was not a success.

Other innovators in heavier-than-air flight were William Hugh Ewen (1879-1947), and the three Barnwell Brothers, Frank Sowter, Richard Harold and Archibald.

William Ewen was a remarkable pilot who distinguished himself during the First World War. Born in Shanghai, the son of Scottish missionary parents from Edinburgh, he took himself to the Blériot School at Hendon where he learned to fly, gaining his Royal Aero Club Certificate No.63 on February 14th, 1911. The first Scot to earn a Royal Aero Club certificate, he returned at once to Lanark and, on August 31st, undertook a double aerial crossing of the Firth of Forth starting from near Portobello to which he was able to return safely after a 12-mile flight taking ten minutes. The following month he went on to plan the opening of Scotland's first flying school at Lanark but found his efforts stonewalled by the authorities. After a short while and not for want of enthusiasm and effort, the Lanark venture failed. It was a sad day for Scotland when the 32-year-old Scot turned his back on his homeland and moved to Hendon where, in partnership with two other Scots, Andrew Mitchell Ramsey and James Hunter, he opened not just a successful flying school but an aircraft factory (The British Caudron Company) where, following a successful tie-up with the French pioneer company, he manufactured large numbers of Caudron aircraft. When the 1914-18 war began, his business manufactured many aircraft under contract for the burgeoning Royal Flying Corps. As his

William Hugh Ewen (1879-1947), the man who opened the first flying school in Scotland at Lanark and failed only to go south and form one of the most important flying schools at Grahame-White's Hendon Aerodrome.

BARRHEAD FLYING SCHOOL. Finest Aerodrome in Scotland. Tuition on Bleriot monoplanes and Farman type biplanes; passenger flights and exhibitions.—SCOTTISH AVIATION Co., 185, Hope Street, Glasgow; or Barrhead, N.B.

The earliest-known advertisement for a flying training school in Scotland. Dating from 1912, this promotes one of two such establishments opened in 1911, the other being at Lanark (Lanark School of Aviation) and opened by W H Ewen. The name Scottish Aviation Ltd is a former incarnation of the name later used by David F McIntyre and Douglas Douglas-Hamilton for their business at Prestwick. This 1911 firm was formed with £10,000 capital by Walter G Duncan, honorary secretary of the Scottish Aeronautical Society. Barrhead Aerodrome, to the south west of Glasgow, opened on June 3rd, 1911, and soon the company had designed its own aircraft. Two aircraft, a biplane and a monoplane, were built by William Mitchell & Sons of Cranstonhill, Glasgow, and, in May of 1911, the former was exhibited at the Scottish National Exhibition. The business also began construction of a four-cylinder engine. Barrhead ceased shortly afterwards following an extensive fire which appears to have destroyed everything of value.

CONTRACTORS TO H.M. ADMIRALTY, WAR OFFICE, AND FOREIGN GOVERNMENTS.

THE BRITISH CAUDRON CO. Ltd.

SOLE BUILDING AND SELLING RIGHTS FOR

Caudron Aeroplanes and Hydro-Aeroplanes

— FOR —

THE BRITISH EMPIRE AND DEPENDENCIES.

OFFICE AND WORKS—
BROADWAY, CRICKLEWOOD.

Cable and Telegraphic Address—
"CAUDROPLAN, CRICKLE, LONDON."
Phone—[illegible] HAMPSTEAD.

As well as forming a highly-respected flying school at Hendon, Ewen secured a licence to manufacture the Caudron biplane in Britain. With two other 'ex-pat' Scots, he founded The British Caudron Co Ltd and became a major supply of aircraft to the military and the newly-formed RFC. After the outbreak of war in 1914, production had to be increased and for a short while Ewen operated a satellite factory and aerodrome at Forthbank, Alloa. Here is a contemporary advertisement for a trade publication in 1912.

business expanded with war contracts, he opened a small satellite factory and airfield at Forthbank, Alloa in Clackmannanshire some 5½ miles east of Stirling. The old aerodrome, long abandoned, was close to the river.

One of those who flew a Ewen-built Caudron biplane in Scotland before the war was George Donald Wilson, a director of the *Edinburgh Evening News*, while the enterprising Lawrence Bell, managing director of the Peebles Motor Company, had a replica of Wilson's Caudron built in his firm's workshops.

Frank Sowter Barnwell (1880-1938) was educated at Fettes in Edinburgh before joining the family business, Fairfield Shipbuilding. However, he soon decamped to Glasgow University, earning his BSc in 1905 and immediately forming Grampian Motors at Stirling with his brother Harold. The third brother, Archibald, operated The Grampian Motor & Engineering Company at Causewayhead near Stirling and would undertake all the subsequent construction work. Frank had seen flying at Cannes and was an immediate convert, building first a glider (which did not fly) and then a succession of three powered aircraft the second of which, powered by a 40 hp flat twin engine made in his company workshop, flew well enough to earn him £50 prize-money for being the first member of the Scottish Aeronautical Society to fly in a heavier-than-air machine. This was the first flight to be made in Scotland by a Scottish-made aeroplane and the date was September 10th, 1909. His next aircraft also won him a prize, this time for being the first to fly a mile in Scotland. That was on January 30th, 1911. Those days, however, if you wanted a career in aviation it was best to bite the lower lip and go south: Barnwell went to The British and Colonial Aeroplane Company at Bristol as chief designer.

Edwin R Mumford and J Pollock Brown were senior employees of William Denny & Brothers' Dumbarton shipyard. Mumford's job was operating the ship test tank and Pollock Brown was his chief assistant. In 1905 Mumford had the idea of building a helicopter powered by a 25 hp Buchet engine and fortunately this aeronautical work was sponsored by Maurice Denny. The machine comprised a lightweight lattice aluminium tubular frame on wooden skids with six large vertical two-bladed screws evolved from the design of a ship's propeller. These 25-feet diameter rotors were designed to revolve at 40 rpm. The engine proved of insufficient power and a four-cylinder inline NEC replacement was also inadequate. Construction took place at the Leven Shipyard, Dumbarton, and following first tests which began in September 1911, the helicopter made a number of tethered flights in 1912. On January 6th 1913, it attained a height of ten feet before a transmission failure resulted in a heavy landing. Late in 1914, a new version was fitted with floats and taxied out onto the water. It then flew a distance of 100 yards ten feet above the waves. This, the first helicopter to fly in Britain, was demolish that self-same might when a gale struck it as it stood on the slipway. Further work was curtailed by the outbreak of war.

There were others who verged on the pioneering spirit, one being Edwin R Mumford and his partner, J Pollock Brown. Both were senior employees of William Denny & Brothers' Dumbarton shipyard. Mumford's responsibility was operating the ship test tank and Pollock Brown was his chief assistant. Their aeronautical work was sponsored by Maurice Denny in 1905. Mumford had the idea of building a helicopter powered by a 25 hp Buchet engine. His machine comprised a lightweight lattice aluminium tubular frame on wooden skids and having six large vertical two-bladed screws evolved from the design of a ship's propeller. These 25-feet diameter rotors were designed to revolve at 40 rpm. The engine proved of insufficient power and a four-cylinder inline NEC replacement was also inadequate.

Built at the Leven Shipyard, Dumbarton, and following first tests which began in September 1911, the helicopter made a number of tethered flights in 1912. On January 6th 1913, it attained a height of ten feet before a transmission failure resulted in a heavy landing. Late in 1914, a new version was fitted with floats and taxied out onto the water. It then flew a distance of 100 yards ten feet above the waves. This, the first helicopter to fly in Britain, was destroyed that self-same might when a gale struck it as it stood on the slipway. Further work was curtailed by the outbreak of war and, although the remains were preserved against post-war revival, the structure was too badly deteriorated and the project was abandoned.

Aside from aircraft, there were also innovations in the field of aero engines that began life in Scotland. The first ever sleeve-valve engine was used by the Argyll Motor Company of Alexandria. Designed by Peter Burt, it powered a number of cars and was a 'world first'. Burt was born in Glasgow in 1856 and lived at 'Hollybank', Silverwells Crescent, Bothwell. In 1898, he approached the manager of Argyll Motors Ltd, John Matthew, with a design for a car engine featuring sleeve valves which would thus eliminate the often noisy conventional valve operating gear. Burt's design was accepted and incorporated into an Argyll car. Production began in 1911. The sleeve valve Burt designed is covered by British Letters Patent Number 1909: 18,140 dated August 6th, 1909.

Nonetheless, the company was unable to maintain commercial success and went into liquidation in 1914. The sleeve valve was forgotten until revived in 1927 by the Bristol Engine Company which made radial aircraft engines. Bristol developed Burt's invention and by 1936 they were in mass production with engines which powered many of the aircraft that won Britain the Second World War.

OTHER EARLY SCOTTISH FLYERS AND TRYERS

Many were those who were attracted to the lure of flight. By the 1930s there were quite a few established flying clubs and people who legitimately built their own aircraft with varying degrees of success. The Flying Flea craze of the mis-1930s saw numerous examples built in Scotland although only two are known to have flown. There were also pre-war Luton Minors built to instructions from the magazine *Practical Mechanics*, but here I really want to record the men who were in a different age – one where nobody quite knew what they were doing, what they should be doing or how they ought best to go about it. These men were as much pioneers as the rest of them, for it was with equal fervour that they sought that will o'the wisp called success.

Early in 1909, the brothers Henry and Alfred Alexander of Edinburgh built a monoplane along the lines of the Demoiselle and this was exhibited at the Scottish Motor Show at Waverley Market in January 1910. The engine was also the work of the Alexanders and developed 20 hp. It had air-cooled barrels with water-cooled heads and was a four-stroke (then known as the Otto cycle). Nineteen feet in span, the complete weight was 140 lbs. There are no reports of flight.

In 1911, the Anderson and Singer Glider was built and successfully flown in Aberdeen. The work of W Anderson and Fred Singer, the Chanute-style biplane had a wing span of 24 feet and a wing area of 288 sq.ft. According to *Flight* (October 21st, 1911) numerous glides between 25 and 30 yards were achieved.

During 1909, the single-seat Baird Monoplane was constructed at Rothesay, Isle of Bute, by a Galloway-born blacksmith named Andrew Blain Baird (1862-1951). He had corresponded extensively with both Cody and Blériot and the finished machine, fitted with an un-named but allegedly Edinburgh-built engine of 24 hp, was styled after the Frenchman's machine. *Flight* (September 17th, 1910) confirms that the aircraft made one flight from the beach, the Baird Monoplane becoming the first Scottish-built heavier than air aircraft to achieve powered flight. The wing span was 29ft, area 180 sq.ft and the empty weight 380 lbs.

The Black Helicopter remains a bit of a mystery. The work of R Black of Mollinsburn and Cumbernauld in 1909, it was powered by two FN motorcycle engines driving a 'multi-blade fan and a two-bladed propeller above the head'. Resembling a strap-on lifting device, the flyer appears to have needed to use his own legs for landing. No flight reports.

G T Cooper was a student at Charterhouse, a public school in Godalming, Surrey, where during his last year he designed and built a glider (February-July 1911). This was tested by towing. On his return to Edinburgh (41 Drumsheugh Gardens) he built and flew a second machine which was later presented to the East of Scotland Aero Club. Cooper became the Hon.Sec of the Edinburgh Aeronautical Society and played a significant part in the early days of Scotland's aviation development.

George Louis Outram Davidson (1878-1939) lived at Banchory, Deeside, where he set up his Davidson Air-Car Construction Syndicate in 1887 and 1898. A high-wing monoplane having a double-decker fuselage to carry 20 passengers and crew, lift was provided by 22 propellers each of six feet in diameter set on vertical axes in the wings. They were to be driven by belts from a power plant in the centre-section. Stability was by pendulum. With a span of 100 feet, a fuselage width of 10 feet and lift equal to ten tons, the Air-Car was an ambitious idea. Model tests took place in Banchory in 1897 and the lift fans were tested by a London-based consultant. Two British Patents were taken out to cover details – 12469/1896 and 13207/1889. Finance for construction was sought but in 1897 the project lapsed. Davidson had mining interests in America and he tried to re-start the project in Denver, Colorado, but by 1908 it had once more faded and the designer returned to Britain.

Wilfred Foulis of Sunbury Mews, Belford Road, was a motor engineer and prominent early Edinburgh motorist who went to Brooklands, Surrey, to learn to fly at the Charles Lane school. He later became Scottish agent for Lane who designed and built several aircraft on his own account. His Foulis Biplane was built in Edinburgh during 1910. A pusher of the Farman type, it was powered by a 80 hp Charron eight-cylinder air-cooled engine driving two propellers 9.5 feet in diameter. The span was 31 feet, wing area 480 sq.ft and the weight 960 lbs.

John Gibson and his son George T Gibson owned the Caledonian Motor & Cycle Works at Leith, and during 1909 they designed and built a wholly-original biplane of the Bristol Boxkite layout and powered by a 30 hp Alvaston water-cooled horizontally-opposed twin-cylinder engine. The 30 feet wingspan aircraft did not fly but provided experience for the Gibson Biplane No.2 which, while having the same engine was somewhat different in detail from the No.1 Biplane. The span was 29 feet and length 30 feet. During August, 1910, the aircraft flew successfully at Beautland Farm, Balerno, making a number of short hops. A third machine followed the same year. Between then and 1914, some nine biplanes were built, one being exhibited at the Scottish International Exhibition of 1911. Work was in hand to build their own engine but the outbreak of war put an end to development and the fate of the aircraft is unknown.

William Crebar was president of the Glasgow Model Aeroplane Club of 101 Vincent Road. *Flight* for April 9th, 1910, reported that the club had a monoplane glider built by Crebar which had flown successfully. Nothing more is known of this.

Nineteen-year-old Robert Dykes Grossart of Milton, Beattock was reported to be making a special monoplane expressly for the Lanark Aviation Meeting of August 1910. A news item in the June 1910 issue of the *Dumfries & Galloway Standard* gave brief details of the machine which would be powered by a 30 hp engine of the constructor's own design. The span was 30 feet. He was a student at the University of Glasgow when the First World War began but he cut short his studies and enlisted in the Cameron Highlanders before being transferred to the Royal Flying Corps as a temporary lieutenant. It was while on flying duties that he was killed on 5th February 1917 when his BE.2c crashed at Beverley, Yorkshire. He was 25.

Charles Hubbard lived at 224 Bruntsfield Place, Edinburgh and was an engineer with the North British Rubber Company. He began his aeronautical work in September 1909 with a machine built around a bicycle and having 240 square feet of wing area. Pedal driven with a 5 feet 3 inch diameter propeller, it weighed 145 lbs and, like others of its ilk, was unsuccessful, The following month, Hubbard made a monoplane with 190 sq.ft wing area and powered by a 60 hp Rex motor. At 260 lbs the machine was probably too heavy to fly but, undaunted, Hubbard built a third machine, a monoplane that was tested at Portobello on June 17th 1911. Described as of Blériot type with a hammock seat, it was powered by two twin-cylinder Rex engines coupled together to drive a 6 feet diameter propeller. Subsequently there was a report that a 30 hp three-cylinder engine of unknown make had been tried as well. No flight details survive.

George Harris Handasyde (1877-1958) was one of the most significant figures in aviation during the first three decades of the 20th century. Born in Edinburgh, he was an early motor-car designer, forming a partnership with Helmuth Paul Martin of Trier & Martin, carburettor-makers, to form the famous Martin & Handasyde aircraft manufacturing company – later known as Martinsyde – at Woking in Surrey. Handasyde designed aircraft in Britain and Australia and his work made a significant contribution to the national war effort in 1914-18.

Joseph Kaufman of Glasgow exhibited a large flapping-wing ornithopter at the Aeronautical Society Show at South London's Crystal Palace in 1868. A steam boiler generated power to flap the wings but, as with most ornithopters, it flapped itself out of contention and fell to pieces.

Little is known of the MacWilliams Glider built at 117 George Street, Whiteinch, Glasgow. It appeared in May of 1911 and was described as being 'of the Valkyrie type' with a span of 30 feet and a weight of 70 lbs.

Even less is known of the Mitchell Monoplane made in Edinburgh and said to have been shown at the Scottish National Exhibition in May 1911.

George William and Stewart Pollock of Robertson Street, Glasgow, built a monoplane during 1910. The large aircraft – wing span was 40 feet – was powered by a 60 hp air-cooled engine made by the Pollocks themselves. There are no reports of it having flown.

The Rathen Biplane was built by three friends to compete in the £1,000 prize for a flight from Edinburgh to Glasgow by a Scottish aeroplane. George Morrice, John Scott and George Dean of Rathen near Fraserburgh built their machine in 1911. Morrice and Scott set up an engineering works at Rathen in conjunction with Dean who was from England and was solely responsible for the engine. The aircraft spanned 22 feet and was to have had an estimated speed of 68 mph but unfortunately Dean had marital problems and 'disappeared' leaving the project in a lurch from which it never recovered. Photographs of the work completed show high-quality workmanship and all major airframe components present.

The Scottish Aviation Company Limited was based at 185 Hope Street, Glasgow, where Frederick Norman designed and built his single-seat *Caledonia* monoplane during 1911. Inspired by Blériot with a nod to Antoinette, the wire-braced monoplane was fitted with a 35 hp JAP engine and flew that November at Barrhead Flying-School in the hands of Robert Wilson Philpott, On December 14th the firm published a prospectus which announced, among other things, the acquisition of Barrhead Aerodrome and an agreement to build Avro-type aircraft, with Alliott Verdon Roe himself on the list of directors. Reports in *The Aero* told of a Scottish Aviation-built Farman-type pusher biplane, already flying, about to be re-engined with a 50 hp Alvaston, built in Glasgow, to allow it to compete for the £1,000 prize on offer for a flight between Edinburgh and Glasgow by an all-Scottish aeroplane. Flying at Barrhead in November 1911 went on with the *Caledonia* and then a further aircraft, a Blériot type with revised undercarriage and a 35 hp JAP engine, appeared. This was called the SAC *Dart* and this, too, seems to have flown well. All ended on April 13th, 1912, when all the aircraft were destroyed in a fire at the Barrhead hangar. After that, nothing further was heard of the company.

The Sirie Monoplane was the work of Marinus Leslie-Miller of 2 Hamilton Street (now Fortrose Street), Partick, Glasgow. He designed an unusual monoplane based on the leaves of the tropical tree that gave it its unusual name. The curved wings were heavily swept back and had considerable dihedral. A scale model was built and flown very successfully on a number of occasions but the full-size machine was never completed.

COMING OF AGE – THE LANARK AIR MEETING

It was a mere handful of years since the Wright Brothers had notched up their flights at Kitty Hawk. The debate about who was the first to fly rumbles on to this day but the popular belief is that they were the first to fly a powered heavier-than-air man-carrying machine in December 1903. In those six years, flying had progressed enormously and Britain was second only to France where virtually all the pioneering pilots in Europe had been spawned. If today we worship pop stars and footballers as virtual deities of their times, in those days it was the names of the pioneer fliers whose exploits were seldom out of the press. Dashing young men with leather coats, goggles and moustaches and backwards-turned cloth caps were the pin-ups of the time.

The newspapers reported eagerly and extensively on the exploits of the airmen at flying meetings being held at places like Hendon, Blackpool and Doncaster. The newly-formed Scottish Aeronautical Society decided it was time for Scotland to get in on the act in a big way and stage a major aerial event. The first aviation meeting to be held north of the Border would run from August 6th to the 13th, so coinciding with the 1910 August Bank Holiday and would take place at Lanark Racecourse.

This was a busy season for what were called air meetings, for July had begun on the third with the big Reims Meeting, quickly established as an annual event and now in its second year. That was followed nearer home by Wolverhampton with a whole week of flying events, followed by one planned at Bournemouth and, within days, another at Blackpool. This last-mentioned was a bit of a disaster, not through the fault of the organisers so much as the local authority which wanted people to spend money on its beaches not gawp at flying machines. Again, there being very few aircraft in the whole of the British Isles, some suggested that aircraft would be a bit thin on the ground, not only in the air. However, since public enthusiasm was at its height, the sight of so much as one aeroplane would satisfy the paying public.

For the pilots, though, it was a bit of a logistics headache. Fortunately in those days if you wanted to take your aeroplane to a flying meeting then the easiest way was to go by train! You took the wings and tail off, put it on a railway wagon – and entrusted it to the oft rough handling of the railway company. Easiest way it may well have been but safest? No way! As happened only too often, red-hot cinders from the engine could and frequently did set following wagons on fire... While only the foolhardy would contemplate flying such vast distances, Lanark was therefore not impossible to get to from Bournemouth, Blackpool or Wolverhampton. You just had to *organise* things properly and then hope for the best.

The Scots, though, had never before organised an aviation meeting and that might well have posed one of those 'first time and last time' scenarios. What actually happened, though, was quite different. By contrast with what had gone before, the Scottish meeting was an exemplary event. Dallas Brett, in his masterful *History of British Aviation 1908-1912*, writes: 'Competent observers stated that the organisation of Scotland's first flying meeting at Lanark surpassed anything which had yet been done in Europe'.

The choice of Lanark as a venue was influenced by three criteria. First the land was reasonably flat and already provided with facilities for accommodating a paying public; second it was accessible by both rail and road links with a railway station just one mile distant; and third there were stables that could accommodate visiting aeroplanes thereby doubling as hangars. In the end, the facilities provided were far and away exceeded as the Caledonian Railway Company quickly built a brand new railway station right outside the main entrance and promised a frequent service of special trains from all directions. A workforce of more than a hundred men spent weeks levelling the ground and removing no fewer than 270 trees and bushes that might obstruct the view of spectators from their enclosures. A 2,000-seat grandstand was built for those who paid 10/- for reserved seats. This had restaurants and refreshment rooms. Of almost equal size was the adjacent 5/- enclosure and beyond that a large 1/- enclosure. New, bright and shiny corrugated iron-clad hangars were erected as it was realised that stables were not really what aviators would expect for their prized machines.

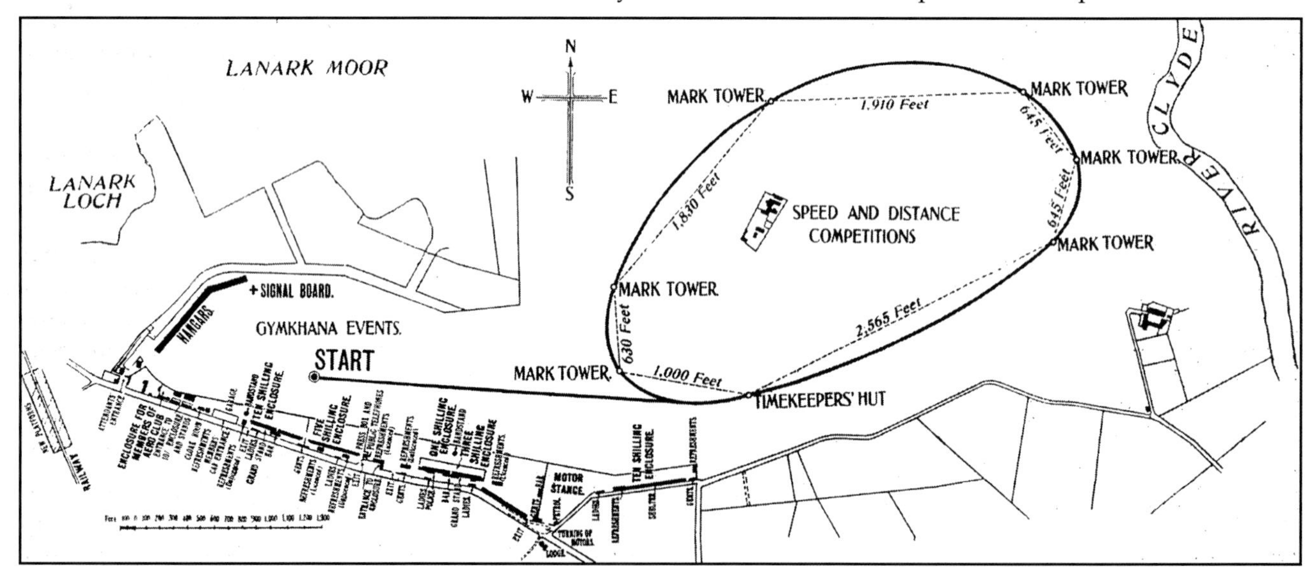

The circuit for the Lanark meeting. The plan was great: the execution not so grand. The new railway station was right outside the main entrance, bottom left, the hangars (still called 'sheds' in those days) were brand new, clean and bright – but the public enclosures were laid out in a strange way. From left to right was, first, the Royal Aero Club members' enclosure, then came the expensive 10/- enclosure followed by the 5/- one and then the 1/- enclosure next to which there was a 3/- one which had its own refreshment area. All these people had a first class view of the aircraft being pushed out, started up, taking off and landing. The actual race circuit was over to the east (right) where it was mostly out of sight of all but the popular majority who had paid their three bob or just a shilling! But the whiff of oil and petrol was strongest at the privileged end! It was, after all, Scotland's first attempt at organising an air show and, as time has told, it not only proved worthwhile but has never been forgotten. The signal board, marked on the plan, was modelled after a cricket score board but stood 40 feet high and was visible from all the stands. The information on contestants, times and events were displayed in letters three feet high.

As already suggested, getting the aircraft there would, at first glance, be simple because they could arrive by railway train. Only the few brave or foolhardy would contemplate actually *flying* to Lanark. You could fly *at*, but not necessarily *to* an aviation meeting! The only problem was that the railways conveyed aircraft on open trucks not in closed wagons. As the locomotives spewed out a goodly mixture of smoke, soot and red-hot coals, the risk of fire was ever-present and often the combustible outcome of travelling through a tunnel which served to focus the sparks.

Of the aviators invited to attend, two had their aircraft damaged in this way and had to have them expensively (and rapidly) rebuilt. A few days earlier, A V Roe, who had been travelling to the concurrent Blackpool meeting, had had his triplane burned up by the railway company near Wigan when sparks had set fire to the tarpaulin covering.

The Lanark meeting opened almost immediately after the Bournemouth meeting on the South Coast at which the Hon Charles Stewart Rolls had so very publicly lost his life. The whole aviation fraternity was still reeling from this catastrophe and race organisers were aware how close to the public poor Rolls was flying when he crashed. At Lanark it was quickly arranged that no aircraft would fly closer than 300 yards to the spectators.

One star of the Lanark meeting Captain Bertram Dickson with his Bristol Boxkite, pictured here. He made history on that occasion by taking the first passengers on a flight north of the Border. Unfortunately he broke his undercarriage on landing but that was such a common occurrence that repairs took little time. Bertram Dickson was an amazing man, a stunning pilot and a man of considerable foresight. Born in Edinburgh in 1873 he learned to fly on a Farman Biplane at Henry Farman's school at Chalone in France taking just six days from April 30th to May 5th 1910. A month later, on June 6th, he notched up his first aviation 'first' with a two hour flight carrying a passenger. He was a captain in the Royal Regiment of Artillery but in September that year he resigned to take up a post with the British & Colonial Aircraft Co flying and demonstrating aircraft. He made the first-ever military flight when he demonstrated to the Army how the Bristol Boxkite could be used to gather intelligence during Army manoeuvres at Larkhill, Wiltshire, and spoke forcefully how the next war would be fought in and from the air. It was largely through his words of wisdom that the Royal Flying Corps was set up. After Lanark he took his aircraft to Milan where once more he set an aviation first, though not one of his choice. On October 2nd he was involved in the first-ever mid-air collision, flying into René Thomas's Antoinette. While Thomas escaped unhurt, Dickson was gravely injured. Although he made well enough to return home and went to work on aircraft design, he never flew again and, on September 29th, 1912, aged 42 years, he died as a result of his injuries. Today if you drive along the lonely A382 past Loch Achanalt in Ross & Cromarty, you will find a prominent white and black road sign pointing up a track to the hillside burial ground of Strath Bran. The board reads 'Grave of Captain Bertram Dickson Pioneer Pilot, Military Aviation'. One of Scotland's greatest flyers lies at peace but shall not be forgotten.

One undoubted star of the show was Edinburgh's own aviator, Captain Bertram Dickson. Dickson had been a captain in the Army, got himself to France where he learned to fly at Maurice Farman's school in six days, and then relinquished his Army career in favour of joining the Bristol Aeroplane Company as pilot, demonstrator, sales person and adviser. He took part in the very first Army manoeuvres at Larkhill in Wiltshire and proved to his military critics that aircraft could be useful in observation and survey. At Lanark he created another 'first' by taking a passenger aloft in his Bristol Boxkite and staying aloft for two whole hours. The crowd loved their fellow Scot and could not have foreseen that in two short years their hero would also be dead, the ultimate victim of another 'first' – this time the first-ever mid-air collision.

The actual event was a landmark success and the representative of *The Aero* (forerunner of *The Aeroplane*) concurred with Dallas Brett when he wrote that it was 'the most successful yet held in Britain'. At that time, however, it had not been appreciated that aircraft had to take off and land into the wind and because of the placing of the timekeeper's box all take-offs had to be made with the prevailing wind which helped produce some impressively long runs in order to become airborne.

Landing circles were placed a few feet in front of the most expensive seats in the grandstand so competitors were forced to land in front of the enclosures regardless of wind direction. It was just this lack of understanding that had contributed to Rolls' death at Bournemouth. As Brett wrote, 'these meetings were organised with both eyes on the turnstiles, and everything was subordinated to the object of giving the populace its money's-worth, quite regardless of the risks involved'. Miraculously, Lanark was not marked by any fatal accidents.

This was the first occasion in the world where aeroplanes had been accurately timed over a straight measured distance and the first world records were established at Lanark covering flights over one mile and one kilometre as timed by official timekeeper Albert Victor Ebblewhite (1871-1939) who would go on to establish a fine career as official timekeeper at many aviation events as well as Brooklands and other motor-racing events.

James Radley, flying a Blériot, achieved 77.67 mph, William Edward McArdle, also in a Blériot, did 72.62 mph while another Blériot, this time flown by the Italian Bartolomeo Cattaneo, managed 72.60 mph. Cecil Grace's Farman did 55.92 mph while George Cyril Colmore's Short made 52.75 mph. At the other end of the scale, Alec Ogilvie won the prize for the slowest circuit, dawdling around in his Wright at just 24.11 mph. Of course, all these records and the numerous prizes, while generating excitement and offering challenge, were really secondary to the true meaning of Lanark, for Lanark only really meant one thing. Scotland could no longer be viewed as an outsider to the flying scene.

ROYAL FLYING CORPS AND THE GREAT WAR

If Lanark was all about the birth of flight, there were other and far more important issues at stake on the broader, national front. These really centred on the love-hate relationship which the Army had with heavier-than-air flying machines. The Army was accustomed to using balloons in which an *observer* could rise up into the sky to observe things like manoeuvres. Thanks to the wonders of technology, he could take up with him a telephone, the wires running back to earth down the cable to which the balloon was securely tethered. This meant that he could speak to the ground from, perhaps, a height of 500 feet or more. You couldn't have that sort of communication from a man in a flying machine, now could you!

But the evidence of successful flight and the potential for wider observation, perhaps even aerial defence if not attack, became harder to ignore. Slowly, grudgingly, the Army changed its tune as the threat of war seemed increasingly real. In some ways, Lanark had forced the hand of the military for one of the early Army pilots was the Scottish artilleryman Captain Bertram Dickson. He became the first Scot to gain an aviator's certificate (Aero Club de France Certificate No. 71, dated May 12th, 1910). Dickson won a major prize at a meeting at Tours, beating French competitors and collecting the Schneider Cup. This was the first important international award gained by a Briton. A month later Dickson flew 61 miles and gained a world duration record – all this while he was officially on sick-leave. On August 3rd, 1910, he left the Army at his own request – on half pay. Although as told elsewhere Dickson's life was to be terribly short, he had proved to his military superiors what could be done with an aeroplane.

Number 2 Squadron's epic flight from Farnborough to Montrose was accompanied by many landings on the way. So unusual was the sight of an aeroplane in those days of peace that any touchdown was accompanied by a major turn-out of the local population. At that time, local photographers were the unsung news journalists of the time and would dash (as best and as fast as they could) to any local event with mahogany and brass plate camera, a leather satchel full of 'double-darks', meaning unexposed photographic plates, wooden tripod and magnesium flash torch. They would record the event, dash back to their studio, develop the plate, title it – and then print it out on post card printed paper. Each was thus an instant real photograph and a post card ready to be sold, written on, stamped and posted. As can be imagined these post cards were not just ephemeral in the extreme (there was only a short time that you could sell 'newsworthy' local cards to the local people before they were old-hat and no longer of appeal) but also very rare. This picture postcard shows Lieutenant Philip William Lee Herbert in his Maurice Farman pusher just after he force-landed in York on February 21st, 1919. The airman's flying kit reveals merely a trench coat and normal Army officer's cap. Among the admiring watchers is a solid and moustached Yorkshire copper, no doubt just as in awe as the be-capped young lads around him.

It began with the Flying Corps Committee of 1911, an enterprise that paved the way towards military aviation. The air wing of the military became the Royal Flying Corps (RFC) and it began trials of suitable aeroplanes. These were conducted under sufferance because many of the Top Brass, brought up with horses, swords and an appreciation of spats, man-servants and brandy, did not 'believe' in them. Led by Old Harrovian Colonel John Edward Bernard Seely, his number two was Glaswegian Brigadier General David Henderson who had served with the Argyll and Sutherland Highlanders. Seely was bold enough to understand his mandate and told his board that 'at the present time in this country we have, as far as I know, of actual flying men in the Army about eleven, and of actual flying men in the Navy about eight, and France has about two hundred and sixty-three, so we are what you might call behind'.

The Committee issued its recommendations. A new independent Service would be set up to be called the Flying Corps which would embrace an Army Wing and a Naval Wing (this would become the Royal Naval Air Service), serving both of which would be a Central Flying School and the Army Aircraft Factory (originally the Balloon Factory at Farnborough) would be renamed the Royal Aircraft Factory. In early April of 1912 the Cabinet approved the proposals and on April 13th King George V officially inaugurated the new service into being with the name Royal Flying Corps.

While the new Service had an uphill task, all credit to Seely, Henderson and the others, they got down to the job quickly, creating a dozen air stations nationwide. The majority were close to military camps in the

The *Daily Mail* newspaper sponsored several 'round Britain' competitions between 1911 and 1914 with the temptation of a £5,000 first prize. This picture, by a local photographer, shows Harry Hawker's Sopwith Tractor Biplane (100 hp Green engine) on its arrival at Cromarty. Hawker had had something of an epic flight. Divided into nine formal stages starting from Southampton, the contest went to Ramsgate (144 miles), then Yarmouth (96 miles); Scarborough (150 miles); Aberdeen (218 miles); Cromarty (134 miles); Oban via the Caledonian Canal (94 miles); Dublin (222 miles); Falmouth (280 miles), and thence back to Southampton (202 miles). The total distance of 1,540 miles had to be covered by each competitor within 72 hours of starting and the attempt, restricted to all-British aircraft, could be made any time between August 16th and 30th. In all there were just four entrants. At 13.55 hrs on August 26th, the waters of Cromarty were reached by Hawker and his engineer, Australian-born Henry Alexis 'Harry' Kauper (1888-1942), who would later end up in charge of Sopwith's aircraft production. Hawker duly left Cromarty and got as far as Dublin where his luck ran out and engine failure forced a sea crash which ended their race. The other competitors had fallen earlier by the wayside and the *Daily Mail*, in recognising that this was the greatest feat of air navigation and pilotage yet achieved by anybody in Britain, generously awarded the gallant Hawker a special personal prize of £1,000. *Picture from the collection of Richard Stenlake.*

south of England but one was to be in Scotland. This was Montrose, the first permanent Scottish military airfield. Of all the military airfields in the British Isles, Montrose was the most outstanding. While Hendon and Farnborough may slip easily off the tongue of memory, their place in aviation history has been established for different reasons. It was in Forfarshire (in 1928 the region returned to its ancient name of Angus) that the first of a dozen nationwide 'air stations' was set up by the British Government to be operated by the Royal Flying Corps. Under the aegis of the First Lord of the Admiralty, Winston Churchill, Montrose was selected for its location to offer protection to Royal Naval bases at Rosyth, Cromarty and Scapa Flow. The first operational military airfield in the whole of the UK was opened on February 26th 1913.

The eventual equipment of RFC Montrose with No.2 Squadron and its aircraft turned out to be an epic event. No.2 Sqdn RFC had been formed out of No.2 (Aeroplane) Company, Air Battalion Royal Engineers at RAE Farnborough on May 13th 1912. It was equipped with a raggle-taggle assortment of aircraft including Bristol Boxkite, a Breguet Biplane, a BE.1, BE.2, a pair of Maurice Farman Longhorns and a Henry Farman Biplane. Allocated to the new station at Montrose, five of these aircraft, all equipped with the 70 hp Renault engine, left Farnborough under the command of Irish-born Major Charles James Burke (1881-1917) who would later distinguish himself in aerial surveillance until his untimely death at Arras. The flight was led by Captain Charles Alexander Holcombe Longcroft as it headed north.

A historic photograph if only for the fact that it is one of the few to survive of the original Montrose RFC base at Upper Dysart Farm before No.2 Sqdn moved north to what would become the proper Montrose aerodrome – Broomfield Farm. The picture shows Maurice Farman S.7 Longhorn No.266 (70 hp Renault). It was flown by Lieutenant P W L Herbert. It crashed on May 5th, 1913 and went to the Royal Aircraft Factory for repair. To the right of this photograph can be seen some of the temporary canvas hangars. *Picture from the collection of Richard Stenlake.*

Completed in a series of stages over the following 13 days, the rather circuitous journey of some 450 miles to Montrose was a litany of forced landings (one of the BE.2 aircraft, piloted by Second Boer War veteran Captain (later Brigadier General) John Harold Whitworth Becke [1879-1949], had to land five times between Sunderland and Newcastle to ask the way because of thick fog) and it was not until February 26th that the first machine landed at Upper Dysart Farm, three miles south of the town. The site, which had been surveyed by the Royal Engineers the previous December, was not ideal and Burke expressed his feeling about the location in no uncertain terms to the Whitehall wallahs.

Without waiting for the heavy brass to spring into action, Burke quickly surveyed the region on his own and selected a better location one mile to the north of the town. Forcing the issue helped and he was sanctioned to move. Dysart Farm was vacated and a fresh base set up at Broomfield Farm where, at the end of the year, the Royal Engineers erected three hangars of Indian Army Shed design on the site (afterwards known as 'Major Burke's sheds'). By the start of 1914, the squadron was in place at its new home. Its stay was to be short-lived for with the start of the 1914-18 war, that August No. 2 Squadron moved to France, Montrose to become the home of the next of many flights throughout its long existence.

The following year Longcroft set up a new British record for a flight in a straight line with a passenger. A long-range fuel tank fitted under the seat enabled him to stay in the air for seven hours 45 minutes and traverse the 389 miles from Farnborough to Montrose in one monumental hop. His passenger was Lieutenant Colonel Frederick Hugh Sykes (1877-1954), Army balloon pioneer and expert and one of Seely's original committee. He would end up as Air Vice Marshall Sir Frederick, a figurehead in the later Royal Air Force.

Longcroft seems to have been fascinated by long distance flight and, on November 22nd 1913 with the entire front cockpit of BE.2c serial number 218 occupied by a 54-gallon additional fuel tank, he flew non-stop from Montrose to Portsmouth and then back to Farnborough, an epic 430-mile flight accomplished in 7½ -hours. For this he was awarded the Royal Aero Club's Britannia Trophy for that year's most meritorious flight.

Before leaving the subject of Montrose, a curious tale is worth relating. During the squadron's relatively short stay at the aerodrome, a fatality occurred in the training regime that was to have an odd outcome. On May 27th, Lieutenent Desmond Lucius Arthur, an Irish-born pilot of some considerable experience, was killed when his BE.2 disintegrated at height and the bits fluttered to earth. All RFC/RAF stations are reputedly ghost-ridden, but Montrose has a reputation for being the most haunted, the unfortunate Lieutenant Arthur being allegedly associated with some of these events.

Pictured on July 25th, 1913, in a field at Monkton, later home of Prestwick Airport, this Bristol-built Royal Aircraft Factory BE.2a, No. 273, was initially issued to No.3 Squadron RFC but re-assigned to No.2 and was one of the five aircraft which made the epic flight from Farnborough to Montrose, this in the hands of Captain Charles Alexander Holcombe Longcroft. Soon after this picture was taken the machine was used by Lieutenant Francis FitzGerald Waldron in three attempts to set a new British altitude flying record and shortly afterwards it went to Ireland for manoeuvres. It was badly damaged on its return flight and was written off on January 17th, 1914.

A respected colleague of mine who was post-war Chairman of BEA, President of the Popular Flying Association and generally level-headed person, Sir Peter Masefield, was airborne in his Chipmunk on May 27th, 1963. En-route near Montrose one fine day he suddenly saw out of the corner of his eye the disintegrating remains of a varnish-strutted biplane fall past him in the sky. So concerned was he that he reported the incident. No aircraft was missing: none had crashed. He remained quietly resolute as to what he had seen.

Although Montrose was an early closure once war had ended, it was recommissioned on January 1st 1936 as No.8 FTS and from then to the end of the Battle of Britain, some 800 pilots were trained. Throughout the Second World War, numerous Royal Air Force and Royal Naval Air Service squadrons served there. Reconnaissance missions to Scandinavia centered on Montrose as did supply-drop missions for the Norwegian resistance movement. As an important and historic military aerodrome it did not escape enemy action and in a raid in October 1940 three Ju.88 bombers did extensive damage and killed five people while injuring many others.

Once the Second World War was over, Montrose became a service and repair station but its lack of hard runways was a limiting factor: it was closed permanently on June 4th, 1952. Today it is the occasional use of private aircraft that disturbs the historic site.

Meanwhile the Naval wing (RNAS) chose Cromarty as the location for the first seaplane station in Scotland. Three aircraft were assigned there and later experiments were conducted at the Rosyth naval base to determine whether it was possible to see submarines from the air. While all this was going on, the first trials were taking place with trying to take off in an aircraft from a ship. This was not impossible for the flat-out speed of a warship was not too far below the speed at which an aircraft could become airborne. Meanwhile William Beardmore & Co of Glasgow patented a special design of ship for naval aircraft. This did not get very far because it incorporated two hangars which, relative to the size of the ship, were vast and not a good use of available deck space. While the theory was fine, the storage of the aircraft on board was not – for the simple reason that nobody had yet thought of building an aircraft with folding wings.

While Naval aviation gradually diverged and followed its own path, land-based activities saw No.6 Reserve Squadron move into Montrose in July 1915 training pilots on the BE.2c. But the winter weather was not conducive to sustained output of pilots, so at the end of December the lot decamped to Norfolk where, they hoped, there would be less wind and rain. The hills were certainly flatter there.

A squadron which later became famed for its achievements and which has at various times been based in well-foreign parts and suffered the ignominy of disbandment (and then been re-formed) is No.43. Formed out of the nucleus of Montrose's No.19 Reserve Squadron and headed up by a proud Scot, William Sholto Douglas, Scotland's second operational squadron was formed in Stirling on April 16th, 1916 with the responsibility of

Home Defence. Its creation was largely due to a particularly unpleasant Zeppelin attack on Edinburgh that April 7th. Thirteen people had been killed by Zeppelin L14 which dropped 4,200 lbs of bombs on the city. Waverley Station was hit as were three hotels and Edinburgh Castle. A whisky warehouse was also targeted.

43's initial home was Fallininch Farm at Raploch – quite close to where the Abbot of Tongland, Damian no less, had attempted flight from James IV's Stirling Castle.

And so Scotland's defences expanded with a new airfield to protect Edinburgh being built at Turnhouse, another at Donibristle in Fife not far from the Rosyth naval base, and a School of Aerial Gunnery opened at Loch Doon, Ayrshire. In the pursuit of better training, the RFC opened No.1 School of Aerial Fighting at Ayr early in 1917.

On April 1st, 1918, the RFC was officially renamed the RAF and that November at the Armistice it possessed 27,333 officers, 263,837 men, 25,400 women (WRAF), 22,657 aeroplanes and 103 airships. Scotland's manufacturers had built more than 2,000 aircraft, ranging from the humble BE.2c to the giant Handley Page V/1500 four-engined bomber. Flying boat hulls had also been produced. Overall it was some contribution to the British war effort.

ROYAL AIR FORCE AND THE SECOND WORLD WAR

The first years of peace saw drastic reductions in the Armed Services, not least the Royal Air Force. By March 1920, 3,260 aircraft remained in 33 squadrons while staffing comprised 3,280 officers and 25,000 men. Of the thirty-odd airfields, representing land bought at market prices, few survived, most having been sold, often back to their original owners, at a loss. Three Scottish airfields remained – Leuchars, Fife, Renfrew (Glasgow) and Turnhouse (Edinburgh).

General Officer Commanding (RFC) Hugh Trenchard was sufficiently experienced in matters of the world to recognise that letting the RAF fade away would be a move from which recovery would be impossible. Hugh Montague Trenchard (1873-1956), 1st Viscount Trenchard, GCB, OM, GCVO, DSO, would eventually end up with the highest rank in the RAF as Marshal of the Royal Air Force. Now in 1925 he formed the Royal Auxiliary Air Force with the establishment of the first four squadrons. The first was 602 *City of Glasgow* at Renfrew, the second 603 *City of Edinburgh* at Turnhouse, and the other two at Northolt (600 and 601). They were joined in 1937 by 612 *County of Aberdeen*.

Two officers of 602 Squadron were the commanding officer, Squadron-Leader Douglas Douglas-Hamilton (1903-1973), Marquis of Douglas and Clydesdale, and the squadron adjutant, Govan-born Flight Lieutenant David Fowler McIntyre (1905-1957). These two men would achieve a 'first' of monumental proportions in 1933 – making a flight over the summit of Mount Everest and taking photographs. They used the Westland Wallace powered by the new supercharged Bristol Pegasus, Sir Roy Feddon's new (1932) supercharged nine-cylinder air-cooled radial engine. Two aircraft would be used and because of Nepalese sensitivity, although RAF machines flown by RAF personnel, they would carry civilian markings, that of McIntyre being G-ACBR (K3488) and that of Douglas-Hamilton G-ACAZ (K4048). On their attempt they would be accompanied by a Gaumont British News cameraman, Sidney R Bonnett. Because of the parlous state of Service funding, the whole event was sponsored by the wealthy, out going and eccentric Lady Lucy Houston (1857-1936).

It is hard to visualise today what an achievement this flight was with the available equipment. Two attempts were made, that of April 19th 1933 being a resounding success achieved by two brave and fearless aviators.

This sort of experience cements relationships and was to prove a significant event for what followed. Two events, ostensibly unconnected, would help shape Scotland's aviation future. The first was the revelation, in 1934, that Britain's air defences were woefully inadequate. The second was when McIntyre and Douglas-Hamilton noticed that a particular part for Ayrshire was curiously free from bad weather for most of the year.

The RAF, with 30,000 personnel, had 732 aircraft operating in 76 squadrons spread throughout the UK. The new defence plans pressed for an increase in frontline squadrons from 41 to 128. More squadrons meant more aircraft but, crucially, highlighted the desperate need for more pilots. The Air Ministry was forced to consider offering contracts for pilot training to private companies. McIntyre and Douglas-Hamilton formed themselves into a company called Scottish Aviation Ltd and set up a training school at Monkton Meadow which happened to be in the middle of that Ayrshire 'sweet spot' they had already detected.

Scottish Aviation Ltd (SAL) tendered successfully for a training contract and Monkton Meadow, first used sporadically in 1913 by No.2 Squadron, became Prestwick Aerodrome. At the same time, Montrose was recommissioned, bought back from its owners at almost twice the price for which it had been surrendered after 1920. Here, in January 1936, No.8 Flying Training School (FTS) was established. And Prestwick became home to No.12 Elementary & Reserve FTS.

While flying training was being built up at Prestwick, Perth (Scone) and Montrose, another Scot was quietly trying hard to locate approaching thunderstorms. Born in Brechin, Angus, Robert Watson-Watt (1892-1973) had begun experiments with his 'cathode-ray tube direction-finders' as early as 1927. One of his stations was at Cupar, Fife. Besides thunderstorms, Watson-Watt could detect and locate sources of radio signals. All this would lead to the development of Radio Direction Finding (RDF) which, by 1938, had been refined into what became known as Radar perfected by Watson-Watt and his team at Bawdsey in Suffolk.

In 1937, work started to build two major military airfields, the first at Kinloss on the Moray Firth. The other was at close-by Lossiemouth. Kinloss was opened on April 1st 1939 and became home to No.14 FTS. Much

Just three and a half miles north-east of Perth lies the aerodrome which, when it first opened in 1936, was known as Scone. Here was founded a flight training school run by Airwork Ltd using a fleet of early-build DH.82A Tiger Moths, many with 'T' serial numbers. This fine study shows fifteen of the aircraft parked on a good day for flying. And there's not a contrail in sight! Airwork acquired the old-established Southern English firm of Air Service Training and moved it to Scone in 1960. Here it flourished until 1996 when it decided to pull out of flight training – a decision rescinded a few years later as the business concentrated on aeronautical engineering and professional pilot training. Scone, today known simply as Perth Aerodrome, is also home to the Scottish Aero Club which was founded in 1927. And once a year it is home to the Heart of Scotland airshow.

later it would become a Coastal Command base and home to Hawker Siddeley/BAe Nimrod aircraft. Lossiemouth opened as No.15 FTS with North American Harvard trainers and Airspeed Oxford twin-engined training aircraft. Later it shifted to Bomber Command and was associated with the famous No.617 'Dambusters' squadron. Lossiemouth was also a Fleet Air Arm station and thence a base for No.8 Squadron with its Avro Shackleton marine surveillance aircraft.

Reverting to pre-war days, Edinburgh's Turnhouse Aerodrome made the news in February 1938 when a Hawker Hurricane, L1555 (one of the first production batch) of No.111 Squadron based at Northolt to the west of London flew from there back to Northolt in 48 minutes. Piloted by Squadron Leader John Woodburn Gillan (1907-41), the Merlin-powered fighter covered the 327 miles at an average speed of 407.75 mph. Gillan was shot down and killed three years later but his unofficial world airspeed record remained to be marvelled at. The aircraft's maximum speed at altitude of 370 mph had been augmented by a strong tailwind.

While talking about Merlin engines, it should not be forgotten that Derby-based Rolls-Royce Ltd had the foresight to open a 'shadow' engine factory at Hillington, Glasgow. The shadow factory plan was managed for the Air Ministry by industrialist Herbert Austin. The importance of Rolls-Royce and, in particular, the Merlin engine, had already led the company to open a new factory in Crewe but production director Ernest Hives was looking for a greenfield site further north that might have easy transport access, an available skilled workforce, and a local authority willing to build the required associated housing. With its easy access to the Glasgow to Paisley railway line, Hillington proved an ideal location and the new factory opened in 1937. The first Merlin engines rolled off the line just two weeks before the start of the Second World War. By 1943 output had reached 400 engines each week, with production peaking at 100 engines in one day, and 1,650 a month. By the end of the war, the plant had manufactured 23,500 new engines during the war, 14% of the total Merlin production worldwide. Managing director Arthur Frederick Sidgreaves later observed: 'If Hillington had not been in existence there would not have been sufficient Merlins to fight the Battle of Britain'. Today that factory is gone, having closed its doors in October 2004, with all production moved to a new facility at Inchinnan next to Glasgow International Airport and a plant at East Kilbride.

Coastal Command has long maintained bases in the north, Sullom Voe in the Shetlands being one of the earliest: it was used during the Great War. The nearby air base at Scatsta created to defend the flying boat base, had the distinction of being the farthest north operational Royal Air Force airfield. This was home to several generations of flying boats from the Saro Londons of 240 Squadron No.18 (Reconnaissance) Group at Invergordon in 1938, to the Short Sunderlands of No.201 Squadron.

During the Battle of Britain (generally defined as from July 10th to September 20th, 1940), Britain's defence was centred on 11 and 12 Group, Fighter Command. Scotland formed part of 13 Group which had its headquarters at Newcastle-upon-Tyne and a sector station at Edinburgh (Turnhouse). At the peak of the battle, Scotland's two auxiliary squadrons, No. 602 and 603, flew their Spitfires south to strengthen the fragile odds. The peak of the battle was September 15th. On that day, RAF losses totalled 26 aircraft, but the Luftwaffe lost 56. That was the day when Nazi Germany realised that Britain was no pushover and put its invasion plans on indefinite hold.

Although the United States was not yet at war with Germany, Lord Beaverbrook's Ministry of Aircraft Production had been forced to seek a boost to aircraft supplies from North America. Bombers were now being flown across the Atlantic on delivery flights via Gander (Newfoundland) and Aldergrove (Northern Ireland). One Lockheed Hudson, lost in bad weather, missed Ireland and made landfall at Prestwick. Immediately recognised as a better location with better weather conditions, the Atlantic Bridge changed its UK end from Aldergrove to Prestwick. Conveniently this destination was on the Great Circle route from Canada which did wonders for navigation from that moment forward. Soon afterwards, the Royal Air Force inaugurated a new division – Ferry Command. This later became integrated into Transport Command as No.45 (Atlantic Ferry) Group.

On August 8th, 1943, an unexpected and unofficial record was set when a Canadian-built Mosquito made the crossing from Gander to Prestwick in five hours and 37 minutes.

Scotland's first-drawn enemy blood of the 1939-45 war occurred very soon after September 3rd's declaration when this Heinkel He.III H-4, coded 1H+JA, was shot down by four Royal Auxiliary Air Force fighters at the end of October. The encounter took place over East Lothian and the twin-engined aircraft, described as 'a scouting plane', came down at Long Newton Farm in the Lammermuir Hills, the location being approximately seven miles south of Haddington and 16½ miles east of Edinburgh off the Humbie-Gifford road. Reports said that two gunners in the Luftwaffe bomber were dead in their seats, a third was alive but wounded twice, and the pilot injured. *The Scotsman* went to town on this maiden incursion into Scottish air space, asserting that 'The Nazi was obviously engaged on a lone reconnaissance, and as soon as he was intercepted he at once responded with sustained bursts of machine-gun fire. At the outset, the bomber endeavoured to exploit the usual enemy flying technique, with which, incidentally, Scots airmen are now becoming familiar. It was unavailing. The Heinkel was harried on all sides by the fighters, and he was relentlessly pursued over the broad fields of the Lothians. He had little chance of escape. Individual aircraft went in to the attack, guns blazing. Their dives might be likened to the 'stoops' of a hawk at an unfortunate quarry. The ground on which the 'plane lay riddled with bullets, is about seven or eight hundred feet above sea level, and commands, a wide view of the Firth of Forth and the Pentland Hills. If the wounded pilot, after he first struck the ground had had any thoughts of rising again he must have been daunted by the sight of the Lammermuirs, which formed a solid barrier in his way. When the news that the bomber had been brought down began to circulate men and women, taken with a desire to see an invading craft at close quarters, made their way on foot or by motor car to the moor, until the scene, with its parked vehicles and the crowd on the knoll above them, had all the appearance of some country coursing meeting. Many of those who gathered about the wrecked machine, which they were prevented from approaching at close quarters by a guard, had seen the concluding stages of the fight. They had followed the chase across country, as if they had been following a pack of hounds.'

Enemy air attacks on Britain did not miss out Scotland and March 13th 1941 saw the first bombing of Clydeside which marked the start of a three-night devastation that killed more than 500 people and crippled industry beside wiping out some 3,000 homes and extensively damaging countless others in this densely-populated region. Air attacks continued at intervals until the last on Scottish soil which was on April 23rd, 1943. Aberdeen was the target – its 34th raid.

During 1943 Moray Firth was the setting for extensive exercises that partly paved the eventual way to the D-Day Landings. They also served as a decoy, for it was anticipated that these would be observed by both enemy aircraft and spies. The exercises were 'leaked' as a practice run for the imminent invasion of Norway. The immediate intention was to deflect enemy resources from what was instead the imminent Allied landings on Italy.

SCOTLAND'S UNWELCOME GUEST

No account of Scotland's wartime aviation history would be complete without reference to the strange and unhappy event of the Second World War – the landing of Adolf Hitler's deputy, Rudolf Hess, on Scottish soil. Rudolf Walter Richard Heß (1894-1987) was the Führer's right-hand man and in 1941 flew himself to Scotland in a Messerschmitt Bf 110 in a personal attempt to negotiate peace with the UK.

The 49-year-old German claimed he acted independently of his Nazi masters and that he carried an important message for the Duke of Hamilton. His destination was Dungavel House where he planned to land, but he got lost in the dark and, realising his predicament, he climbed to 6,000 feet and baled out, landing at Floors Farm on Eaglesham Moor, Renfrewshire, where he was discovered by local ploughman, David McLean, injured and struggling with his parachute. His aircraft crashed at 23:09 hrs on May 10th, some twelve miles west of Dungavel House. Meanwhile the duke, a wing commander at RAF Turnhouse, was away from home on duty. It had been his station that was one of those tracking the erratic course of Hess's flight over Scotland. The following day Hamilton and Hess met.

What actually happened at that meeting has never been divulged and the many widely differing accounts might suggest some sort of conspiracy, one thought being that had Hess been successful in negotiating a peace treaty between Britain and Germany (meaning a declaration of neutrality), Churchill would have failed in his negotiations to try to get America to enter the war in Europe. In Germany, Hess was seen as having betrayed Hitler and was therefore branded a traitor.

He fared little better with the Allies: he was taken prisoner and eventually tried for war crimes for which he served a life sentence. Hess's war crimes were debatable and many felt his incarceration in Berlin's Spandau jail (in the end he was the very last remaining inmate, the building being demolished the moment he was dead) both cruel and inhumane.

The speculation over Hess, his intentions, the contents of his papers and the Whitehall cover-up that led to his incarceration and ultimate death in captivity, is a grey area in which Scotland played an unhappy if innocent part. Portions of his aircraft, Serial number 3869, code VJ+OQ, are now exhibits in London's Imperial War Museum.

Gloster Meteor F.8 WA849 was one of the aircraft operated by No.43 Squadron, known as The Fighting Cocks, at Leuchars in 1949. At that time there were two similar Fighter Command units at the base – 43 and 222 – and both flew the F.8 and practised arch inter-squadron rivalry. The emblem of 43 Squadron was a cockerel with the motto 'Gloria finis', loosely translated as 'The thing that finished off Gloria'. On a patch of grass outside the squadron commander's office in the flight hangar was a small chicken run with a pet cockerel in it which crowed proudly when the crew arrived each day. One morning it didn't greet us but sat there grey, silent and clearly ashamed of its looks. 'Treble-Two' had been over during cover of darkness and blanco'd it! Only after a good wash did our bird crow again. A week later, Treble-Two arrived one morning to find their hangar and offices daubed with a curious message in whitewash. 'Koureni Zakazano' it read. It was everywhere – office doors, windows, the hangar itself. Nobody knew what it meant but the worst was feared. Treble-Two's squadron commander went to great lengths to find out what it was and who had done it. In those pre-Internet days, there was no easy way of checking the meaning, but the culprits were assumed to be 'the Fighting Cocks' of 43 Sqdn. It took many weeks before somebody found out the words were Czechoslovakian for 'Smoking prohibited'. Nobody could be 'had' for painting a valid warning sign on RAF property and there the matter quietly rested – but there followed many a knowing look in the Mess…

SERVICE FLYING INTO MODERN TIMES

For the first 35 years after the end of the Second World War, Britain and America together battled the war that few now recall – the so-called Cold War. It began almost as soon as the war with Germany ended in 1945 and went on into the 1960s. Events such as the Cuban Missile Crisis and the Nuclear Arms Race all meant that the allies (Britain and the US) feared an attack or other form of incursion from the Soviet Union. The threat of nuclear attack was felt very real and as a result both nations prepared for an 'imminent' challenge from the Soviets.

For their part, the Soviets persisted in provocative actions. Vast surveillance bombers capable of carrying missiles made frequent incursions into UK airspace and these had to be monitored and defence aircraft had to be scrambled to force them to turn round and head back for home. While there was no doubt that either side were fully armed and could have made a 'hot challenge', such an act would have provoked war. It was a delicate situation and Britain's defence now shifted almost entirely into Scotland where fighter squadrons remained on 24-hour alert and surveillance aircraft patrolled the Eastern skies endlessly.

All of this was conducted from fields such as Leuchars in Fife and Lossiemouth in Moray with others actively serving as back-up and supply bases. Thankfully, the Cold War finally fizzled out as common sense prevailed, but those were tense days and Scotland was the UK's front-line defence. On top of this virtual war-footing were the search and rescue missions monitored by Hawker Siddeley Nimrod aircraft. These maritime patrol aircraft were developed from Britain's first pure-jet airliner, the de Havilland Comet. They were introduced in the early 1970s to replace the aged and obsolete (but much-loved) Avro Shackletons, themselves derived from the war time Lancaster bomber. Many Nimrods were based in Scotland, predominantly at Lossiemouth, until, in 2011, some lunatic at Whitehall decided that they should all be scrapped. Perfectly good aircraft, some newly-overhauled at huge expense, were chopped up and melted down. All this did was to confirm the popular feeling amongst ordinary people that lunacy reigns in the corridors of power.

RAF Leuchars has been a front-line fighter station since the war years and accordingly has been home to many top squadrons. Here is an English Electric BAC F.6 Lightning of 74 Squadron which was resident at this east coast field from March 1964 until June 1967. It re-equipped with this aircraft in November 1966.

Today the two most important Service airfields, in descending order of squadron occupancy, are Leuchars and Lossiemouth. In the past key centres have included Abbotsinch, Donibristle in Fife (both Fleet Air Arm repair depots), Prestwick (flying training), Montrose and Renfrew which was the European end of the Trans-atlantic sea ferry where knocked-down Canadian and American-built aircraft were shipped to King George V Dock at Govan and then transported to the airfield for assembly, inspection and delivery flight across the UK. The flying boat bases in Orkney and Shetland have also faded from the scene as maritime flying now employs ultra-long-range land-based aircraft rather than waterborne craft such as the once-familiar Sunderlands.

Stalwart military aircraft that have been Scottish-based guardians of the British soil have come and gone. Sunderland, Shackleton, Nimrod – names that were once familiar to all are now mere history. Fighter bombers have also come and gone – Meteor, Hunter, Phantom, Jaguar, Tornado – as some wit once said 'all of the noise but none of the grace of the old-timers'. Still, occasionally, a Spitfire roars through the Highland skies to remind the very old of the old days and to inspire in the young the ever-present importance of preserving our history into the future.

THE BEGINNINGS OF A COMMERCIAL AIR SERVICE

There had been a few disparate attempts at establishing passenger air services in Scotland during the late 1920s and early 1930s but it was not until 1933 that things really happened. The formation of Highland Airways by entrepreneur Ted Fresson spearheaded a revolution in a communications network hitherto operated by boats that sailed at the whim of the weather.

Ernest Edmond Fresson was the pioneer of Scotland's air services that offered a speedy link between the islands and the mainland. Although born in Hampstead, North London, in 1891, he devoted his flying career to opening up communications between the isolated and geographically-challenged communities of the Scottish Islands. He set up his own company, Highland Airways Ltd, becoming both its managing director and chief pilot. He conducted a search for the best-possible aircraft to suit the routes he wished to operate and found Helmut Stieger's prototype ST-3 Monospar, a demonstrator to show off the designer's unusual but clever lightweight airframe structure. He had to wait while the fledgling Croydon-based General Aircraft Company set up its production line before he could acquire what would be a ST-4 Mk.II Pobjoy-powered twin-engined four-seater Monospar. Registered G-ACEW, he named it *Inverness*. Here he is seen in typical pose with his new aircraft outside the Monospar factory. *Picture from the Richard Riding Collection.*

Without Captain Ernest Edmund 'Ted' Fresson's pioneering work in the establishment of communications in the Highlands and Islands, Scotland's airline development and expansion would certainly have taken a different path. Fresson (1891-1963) was born in Hampstead, North London, yet was to become the most important figure in the development of Scottish commercial aviation and devoted his life to creating air connections for outlying communities.

Places like Caithness, Orkney and Shetland owe him an immense debt of gratitude as indeed do the Western Isles. It was he who first found an aerial way to Wick where, on April 19th, 1931, he landed his de Havilland Gipsy Moth G-AAWO in a field on Barnyards Farm. His business partner, who also happened to own the aircraft, was Miss Helen Pauer who flew with him that day. The following day, Sunday 20th, they flew on to Kirkwall where, after circling the town looking for a field, they landed next to the Balfour Hospital. Here they were greeted by Ian McClure, Orkney's surgeon who, like Fresson, was a First World War veteran. McClure had lost a leg in the war but that did not prevent him from driving Fresson around Kirkwall looking for a more permanent field.

Fresson recognised both the need for air transport in the Northern Isles and the opportunities it would bring. Highland Airways, registered in Edinburgh on April 3rd, 1933, began operating air services between Inverness (Longman Airfield) and Kirkwall in Orkney. The service officially started on May 9th, 1933. Mrs Macdonald, wife of the Inverness Provost, christened the aircraft with a bottle of whisky naming it *Highland Dew*. Later the service was extended to bring in Caithness using suitable field landing sites on the outskirts of Wick and Thurso.

A local diarist later recorded:

> I do not remember Stronsay before Fresson when our only service out was by slow steamer. For me he seemed to have always been there. His aeroplanes in 1934 brought to a people who had previously travelled at the fastest by horse and gig, the thrills of hurtling through the air at a hundred miles an hour or more. Fresson's air service to Stronsay beat my father's first motor car by a year.

Fresson himself, writing in his memoir *Air Road To The Isles*, related that 'the natives of the outlying islands took to this new form of transport as ducks take to water'.

All did not go well for Fresson, however. Devoted as he was to his goal of linking up Scotland's isolated communities, there were others who challenged his monopoly. Prime amidst these was Gandar Dower who created his own airline to challenge the pioneering Fresson.

A small and otherwise insignificant picture-story in the London *Evening News* for Monday, March 19th, 1934, hides a tale that has never before been revealed. Airspeed was promoting its AS.5 Courier, an all-wood single-engined six-seater with retractable undercarriage designed by Alfred Hessell Tiltman. Anxious to find a suitable aircraft for his projected Scottish Islands air service, 43-year-old Ernest Edmund Fresson went to Croydon to see the aircraft but was immediately put off by its size and the complexity of the landing gear. While there he caught sight of the General Aircraft ST-3 Monospar, G-AARP, and at once knew he had found the aircraft he wanted. But it was only in prototype stage and being used as company demonstrator: he had to wait almost a year for G-ACEW to be built for him. Meanwhile, the Portsmouth-built Courier was snapped up by the fledgling North Eastern Airways which would go on to open a service between London and Newcastle, Edinburgh, Perth and Aberdeen. The newspaper captured an early proving flight but the service (which in the end did not include Glasgow) did not start until the following year.

P MONDAY. The Evening News MARCH 19, 1934

BY AIR TO GLASGOW

A plane ready to leave Croydon to-day for Glasgow to try out a new service which is expected to begin in six weeks.

Eric Leslie Gandar Dower (1894-1987) was a Unionist Party politician and entrepreneur who saw a business opportunity in aerial communications in Scotland. Determined to be top dog he strove to compete with pioneers such as Fresson and eventually either take them over or put them out of business. He registered his business Aberdeen Airways Ltd in Edinburgh on January 2nd, 1934 as a private company with a capital of £8,000. In 1937 the name would be changed to Allied Airways (Gandar Dower) Ltd.

Airline operation at this time was almost exclusively devoid of aids such as blind flying instrumentation and radio. And when radio was installed, the extent of its use was governed by whether or not there was an operating radio station within reach. When aviation ground radio installations were created, radio communications were conducted on 826 meter frequency which meant that messages could be picked up by ordinary people on the lower end of the Long Wave spectrum of their domestic receivers. It was said that this was used by people so they knew when an aircraft was coming in and, particularly, who was flying it. Eric Starling provides an excellent account of the installations and the limitation of the system:

> All aircraft had fixed aerials running from wingtips to the rudder. As we were using a frequency in the 800 meter bracket, this did not give much range and was only used close to the airfield. In the flight deck was a reel containing 100 feet of wire with a lead weight on the end. This was the 'trailing aerial' and it gave adequate range. However there was no future in trailing 100 feet of copper wire through a thunderstorm. One just short circuited the storm. Therefore I had to keep my trailing aerial wound in so my radio was therefore useless.

It was the unlikely operation of Railway Air Services which evirtuated on Scottish air travel and showed what might be done. Founded by the railway companies as their own answer to the challenge of regional air transport (which was initially viewed as a foul competitor to the train services), the business was set up in January 1934 with offices in a single room on a top floor at London's Victoria Bus Station. The directors represented the Great Western Railway, the Southern Railway, London, Midland and Scottish Railway and the London & North Eastern Railway. To impart some aeronautical credence to these high-powered steamers, the fifth director was Lieutenant-Colonel Harold Burchill who represented Imperial Airways. Operating base for the newly-formed business was London Airport, Croydon, and its first aircraft was G-ACPX, a de Havilland DH.84 Dragon.

Scottish Airways Ltd's de Havilland DH.89 Dragon Rapide G-ADAJ, registered June 5th, 1935, stands in isolation at Sumburgh Aerodrome, the one-time Sumburgh Links situated right at the very southernmost part of Shetland. Surveyed by Fresson early in 1936, the aerodrome opened for use on June 3rd that year. Later it was expanded for the RAF during the war and hard runways were laid. It formed the base of 404 Squadron equipped with Bristol Beaufighters. Today it is served by Loganair. The Rapide seen here survived the war to be sold to France in 1947. *Picture from the collection of Richard Stenlake.*

One of the fledgling airline's key assets was not just the ability to tie in with the railway company's timetables, but its valuable contacts with the General Post Office and the possibility of aerial mail contracts. The initial services were between London and Cowes (Somerton) on the Isle of Wight but soon extended to Southampton, Plymouth, Teignmouth, Bristol, Cardiff, Liverpool and Birmingham.

A golden opportunity came in July and August of 1934 with plans to establish a LMS-sponsored trunk air route between Glasgow and London operated in conjunction with Imperial Airways. Three DH.86 10-passenger four-engined airliners were ordered from de Havilland. These were the short-nosed single-pilot versions of the Express (as it came, unofficially, to be known) as distinct from the twin-pilot variants first supplied to Australia and were named *Mercury* (G-ACVY), *Jupiter* (G-ACVZ) and *Delphinius* (G-ACPL). Monday, August 20th, 1934, saw the opening of a new route, Glasgow-Belfast-Manchester-Birmingham-London, with a frequency of once in each direction per week day.

Although the route achieved a remarkably high rate of reliability in spite of often adverse weather conditions, all was not well for these early commercial operations. The October 1934 report of the Superintendent to the Board of Railway Air Services included a telling passage:

> Practical experience of operating air services in this country indicates that the greatest difficulty confronting the operator is in respect of ground facilities. In the case of Railway Air Services we can state definitely that the aerodromes which we are using are, with the exception of Croydon, inadequate for regular operation of fast commercial aircraft.
>
> Airport authorities have not been able to keep pace with operators, in particular those utilising high-speed aircraft, and unless some definite action is taken by the Government to obtain co-ordination of policy between Municipalities and the Air Ministry (as representatives of the operators' interests), irrecoverable damage will be done to the industry as whole, as the Municipal Authorities will be loath to incur further expenditure for the provision of additional land and facilities required for safe operation.

Clearly RAS was not accustomed to operations from the tiny grass strips that the Scottish airline pioneers such as Edmund Fresson and Eric Gandar Dower would have considered being par for the course. RAS was, after all, an off-shoot of the railway companies and Imperial Airways – organisations that were perhaps a little inflexible when it came to the thought of marginal operating conditions. And even Glasgow's Renfrew, it has to be admitted, was a bit primitive by Croydon standards in 1934.

By the end of 1934, London was connected to Scotland via the combined services of RAS and Hillman's Airways, the latter with the Postmaster-General's mail contract since Hillman had tendered lower than RAS for the Christmas mail.

Although Railway Air Services was a good idea at the time, there were problems. Buying an air ticket at the railway station was fine, but the railways prohibited travel agents and other ticketing sources from handling their routes – a prohibition not lifted until 1938. That was not all. The daily flight from Glasgow to London took five hours and 40 minutes because the traveller had to go via Belfast, Liverpool, Manchester and Birmingham. By the autumn of 1935 it wasn't even a through trip and the Glasgow-bound passenger, on leaving London, would have to change in Belfast for a connecting flight.

After Fresson had seen his ground-breaking airline operations usurped by others, he continued to press for Scottish improvements. One of these was the creation of Britain's very first hard-surface, tarmac runway. It was in 1940 that the Admiralty developed Hatston, a mile outside Kirkwall, as a four-runway airfield. Because of the low-lying muddy ground, Fresson suggested laying tarmac runways, something never before done in Britain. Shortly afterwards two Fleet Air Arm squadrons took up occupancy – 771 Fleet Requirements Squadron equipped with Fairey Swordfish, and 800 Squadron with its Blackburn Skuas. On April 10th, a flight of Skuas engaged the German cruiser *Königsberg* and sank it. On October 2nd, 1940, in the best naval tradition of naming demonstrably unfloatable objects as if they were things seaworthy, Hatston became HMS *Sparrowhawk*. After the war, it reverted to airline use with BEA but was deemed too small for the DC-3 Pionair aircraft and was closed in favour of the new airfield. Hatston served as home to the Orkney Flying Club between 1953 and 1957 after which it became an industrial estate. But it was still Fresson's first hard-runway'd field!

The American-built Consolidated B-24 Liberator was one of the key long-range aircraft used by the Royal Air Force. As the bomber produced in the greatest quantities anywhere in the world, the Liberator was not without its faults. While more up-to-date than the better-recalled Boeing Flying Fortress, its controls were heavy and poorly harmonised. Intentionally light-weight construction combined with the multiplicity of fuel tanks spread throughout the airframe gave the Californian-made heavy-lift aircraft an unhappy reputation of readily catching fire when attacked and breaking apart and then catching fire easily when crashed. At the end of the war there were a lot of them around and Scottish Aviation, which had been servicing them on the RAF/BOAC Transatlantic Ferry Service for some years, saw a possibility to convert them into stop-gap airliners. Known as the LB-30A, the passenger ferry aircraft of the war years offered Spartan accommodation for five crew and seventeen passengers. While BOAC itself undertook some passenger conversions, the majority were carried out at Prestwick where self-sealing fuel tanks were fitted, all military gear removed and a passenger cabin created with sound-proofing and upholstered seats. With the removal of nose weaponry, a more pleasing rounded proboscis was possible. Five such aircraft were used by Scottish Airlines and this one, G-AHZR (formerly AL552) received its C of A on September 30th 1946. Operated as a 24-seater deluxe airliner, it served well until being sold to Hellenic Airlines in November 1949 where it became SX-DAB. This picture is taken of the aircraft flying over Prestwick in 1946. *AMG Archives.*

AIRLINE DEVELOPMENTS SINCE THE WAR

Post war aviation on internal routes was to a considerable extent governed and influenced by the new airline set up on January 1st, 1946 – British European Airways Corporation, known simply as BEA. It was set up through the aegis of the Civil Aviation Act, 1946, 'with a view to providing civil air services in various parts of the world and in particular in Europe (including the British Islands).' The first part of this specification was met with the establishment of BOAC and its South American companies. The second part was a sort of formalised Railway Air Services although, as regards the British Islands, BEA never serviced the Isle of Wight.

While BEA's fleet of converted Dakotas and Vikings flew from the company base at London's Northolt Airport to various close-by parts of Europe and Scandinavia, the challenging services above Glasgow were, if not exactly eschewed, seen by the London bosses as burdensome. But BEA's mandate had absorbed both staff and aircraft of the wartime Associated Airways Joint Committee and swallowed up the Scottish airline companies and their routes. Those absorbed comprised Allied Airways (Gandar Dower); Channel Island Airways; Great Western & Southern Airlines; Highland Airways; Isle of Man Air Services; North Eastern

Airways; Railway Air Services; West Coast Air Services, Scottish Airways, and Western Isles Airways. As the new owners of such well-established, fine businesses one might have expected co-operation and credit, compassion and appreciation for past service. Far from it! BEA saw the regional inland and island services as a pain in the backside. Unsympathetic would be an understatement. The old brigade, including founders like Fresson and other highly experienced men, were all fired.

It is to be regretted that BEA developed a senior management structure essentially hostile to existing airline operations. When set up on January 1st, 1946, it took over routes from 110 Wing, RAF Transport Command. The Chairman was the affable 67-year old Brigadier General Sir Harold Brewer Hartley (1878-1972), a chemist by learning and pre-war chairman of Railway Air Services who was already somewhat past his 'sell-by' date. His number two was the ebullient if eccentric Whitney Willard Straight (1912-79) who was a keen amateur flyer, a racing driver and a general all-round enthusiast and hence too good to last long in office. As managing director was the significantly incompetent and unpopular Gerard d'Erlanger (1906-62). Gerard John Regis Leo d'Erlanger, CBE, was a chartered accountant by trade and, at the outbreak of war, had been in charge of the Air Transport Auxiliary (ATA).

Initially BEA worked acceptably well and the so-called Scottish Division, headed by George Nicholson who had run, among others, Scottish Airways Ltd until merged into BEA, was sustained. In the summer of 1947 everything changed when both Hartley and Whitney Straight were shifted sideways to run BOAC to replace Viscount Knollys (Edward George William Tyrwhitt (1895–1966)). This left d'Erlanger in sole charge of BEA – not a particularly good development. The main problem was that BEA's new management did not understand Scotland and its island community needs. Come to that, it didn't really seem to understand airline operations. Not that BEA failed – it certainly lost money during its first two years – but its style did not go down well, especially in Scotland.

British Caledonian was launched in September 1971 with a huge celebration at, of all places, London's Gatwick Airport. Keen to maintain its origins the airline established its own pipe band which enjoyed considerable success in both Renfrew and 'down South'. Here we see the band posing at Gatwick in front of BCAL's Boeing 707 349C, G-BAWP which the airline acquired from Eire on April 24th, 1973 where it had been EI-ASO. Two years later it was returned to Ireland where it resumed operations under its old registration. In 1988, BCAL became part of British Airways and one sad casualty of this change of direction was the break-up of the pipe band.

Perhaps it was only to be expected but almost as soon as d'Erlanger took office his first task was to eviscerate the Scottish Division. He announced its September closure and the consequent redundancy of both Nicholson and Ted Fresson. Everything beyond Glasgow and Edinburgh would go. The ensuing uproar echoed not just through Scotland but percolated down to the corridors of Whitehall. In March 1949 came the news that 42-year-old d'Erlanger had been sacked by Lord Pakenham the Civil Air Minister. What was needed – and quickly – was a 'safe pair of hands' and that came in the form of Lord Douglas of Kirtleside better known as Marshal of the Royal Air Force Sir Sholto Douglas. He successfully put some of the pieces back in place and it was when Peter Masefield (1914-2006) took over the reins in 1950 that BEA would take its proper place in the airline industry. By then, though, most of the damage had been done and BEA had established itself as having ridden rough-shod over all and sundry. Both d'Erlanger and my friend Masefield ended up with knighthoods, one for creating mayhem and the other for straightening it out, perhaps?

Initially, BEA was content to push its inherited fleet of Dragon Rapides around the Scottish Islands although it would have made better economic sense (to the people in London's Keyline House – BEA's headquarters) to standardise their fleet on Dakotas and Vikings. The fact that these aircraft were unsuited to the terrain and airstrips was a mere administrative nuisance...

Over the years that followed two things happened to cement Scotland's internal air services. First was the gradual and inevitable dismantling of the BEA 'monopoly' terminating in the absorption of BEA into the newly-formed British Airways on April 1st, 1974 (curiously 50 years to the day since the formation by an earlier airline amalgamation of Imperial Airways). Second has been the establishment of a robust and independent air service.

This really began in 1946 when Scottish Aviation Ltd formed Scottish Airways (Prestwick) Ltd and rapidly engaged itself in world wide cargo and as an Armed Forces trooping carrier. By the time it ceased operations in 1960 (its fleet and routes went to Dan-Air), a new mould had been cast.

There have been numerous other attempts to create airlines in Scotland since the war, successful ones like Caledonian (later British Caledonian) and several with similar titles such as Scottish Airways and Scottish Airlines have rubbed shoulders with others that have long been forgotten such as Highland Express, Scotcourt, Eastern Seaboard and a host of other small charter operators.

One that has lasted is Loganair founded in 1962 as a subsidiary of the Duncan Logan Construction Company. Acquired by the National Commercial Bank of Scotland in 1968 (the following year this merged with the Royal Bank of Scotland) it benefitted from British Airways' route rationalisation programme which saw the transfer of its low-density Scottish routes to Loganair. The scheduled network was expanded serving Shetland, Orkney and the Western Isles comprehensively from Glasgow and Edinburgh. The company also began a service to Londonderry in Northern Ireland and then took over the former British Airways Belfast-Edinburgh service.

Today Loganair is an indispensable link between Scotland's more distant communities bringing the ability to commute to those for whom the sea seemed an eternal barrier.

One aspect of Scottish air operations which is uniquely vital to the nation is the air ambulance service. Emergency flights had been carried out as early as the 1930s. Indeed the first such flight is recorded as having taken place on May 14th 1933 when Captain Joseph Harold Orrell flew Midland & Scottish Air Ferries' Dragon G-ACCZ to rescue an Islay fisherman suffering acute stomach pains and suspected peritonitis. Since that time, increasing numbers of 'mercy flights' have been made, one notable mission being the air lift to Edinburgh Royal Infirmary of the lighthouse keeper at Eshaness near Hamna Voe, Shetland, who was said to be so seriously ill that he would not survive a long sea and road journey.

These flights provided a facility that was of considerable importance to the Islands but it was not until 1947 when the air ambulance service was officially recognised. Two events that year cemented both its existence

G-BEDZ registered on August 25th 1976 was a Britten-Norman Islander which joined the Loganair fleet in November 1977. It had first been sold in Canada and registered C-GYUG on August 25th, 1976. With Loganair it initially bore the name Captain David Barclay MBE but this was changed later to Captain Eric A Starling FRMetS in honour of the pioneering airline pilot who, along with Fresson and Neilan, got the inter-islands air services up and running for Scotland. On May 19th, 1996, while engaged in a Medicare flight in bad weather, it was destroyed in a fatal accident at Tingwall, Shetland.

and its financial sustainability. The first was the formation of the National Health Service which allocated the funding of the service to the then Department of Health for Scotland and the second was the arrival of British European Airways (BEA) as successors to the previous independent Scottish airline operators. The new operator sustained the service until 1973 when the operation was taken over by Loganair.

Vital to the operation of any service is the availability and development of airfields. Scottish Aviation realised that although Prestwick was some distance from the centre of Glasgow, it could be reached by rail in a shorter time than a city centre taxi might make Renfrew or Abbotsinch in the rush hour so it renamed its base as 'Glasgow-Prestwick' which is no less outlandish than more recent bandwagon-jumpers in the south who have re-named Oxford Airport as 'London-Oxford', Southend as 'London-Southend' and have even proposed 'London-Schiphol'.

Scotland's opportunity for a new 'central' hub came as early as 1928 when the Falkirk, Grangemouth and East Stirlingshire Publicity & Development Association was formed to find ways of bringing investment into the area. The chairman was Christian A Salvesen of the eponymous shipping company and he looked at air communication. On July 24th, 1930, an improvised aerodrome was set up at West Mains, Grangemouth, and the occasion of a visit by the popular director-general of civil aviation Sir Sefton Brancker used for the provision of an ad hoc air display by visiting aircraft. On hand to co-ordinate things was Scotland's premier advocate for civil aviation – the Marquess of Douglas and Clydesdale, Squadron Leader Douglas Douglas-Hamilton who at that time was also MP for East Renfrewshire. This was a bold and brave move for the Depression that followed the Wall Street Crash of 1929 was beginning to affect Scotland.

An airfield at Falkirk seemed likely but precious few suitable sites could be found. That September 13th, 1930, an air pageant was staged at Earl's Gates described as 'the most spectacular display staged in Scotland'. It was opened by Salvesen. The following year, Monday September 28th saw Captain C D Barnard's Air Circus visit Falkirk's Reddoch Farm. Charles Douglas Barnard was the original 'Flying Circus' operator and toured the British Isles with his aeronautical show.

Scottish Aviation Ltd had been formed in 1935 with its Prestwick Aerodrome on the Ayrshire coast. Now things were expanding with Air Ministry training contracts likely, SAL's founders (David Fowler McIntyre and Douglas Douglas-Hamilton) began the search for a suitable field to develop in the east. Edinburgh's Macmerry Aerodrome near Tranent was a close contender but with the recommendations of the Maybury Committee openly in favour of a single aerodrome to serve the interests of both Glasgow and Edinburgh, the Falkirk-Grangemouth area was back in the running. This issue was more or less settled when the Air Ministry proclaimed the gradient at Macmerry too great for pilot training.

Grangemouth suddenly ticked all the boxes and the original site was expanded to 520 acres, embracing six farms and the greater part of the golf course. Air Ministry approval for the site was received on February 2nd, 1939 and work proceeded immediately. The new Central Scotland Airport was to become a reality. Equidistant from Glasgow and Edinburgh, it offered excellent all-weather approaches up the Forth and was virtually flat with few obstructions.

Although far from finished, the first commercial service was a DH.89a Dragon Rapide of North Eastern Airways from Perth which landed on April 22nd, 1939. By May No.35 ERFTS was installed, together with its DH.82 Tiger Moth aircraft and RAF training began in earnest. At the same time, the airfield was promoted as Edinburgh Airport (Grangemouth). It was officially opened on July 1st by Marshal of the Royal Air Force Viscount Hugh Montague Trenchard (1885-1935).

Just a few short months later, on September 3rd, 1939, the Royal Air Force assumed sole control of Grangemouth. Soon it was home to operational units including No.58 Operational Training Unit.

With its grass runways replaced by 1945 with concrete, Grangemouth saw out the war and survived into peacetime but besides being a temporary home to No.13 Reserve Flying School and its Tiger Moths as well as No. 2 Gliding School with its Slingsby Kirby Cadet and Grunau Baby gliders, it was ignored in the overall picture of Scotland's post-war flying needs. In November 1948, the Air Ministry relinquished its interest in the site and the local authority quickly stepped in with a view to local housing and industry. What had all-too briefly been Scotland's largest airfield was scrapped. Today the site is the location of Grangemouth Oil Refinery.

AIR TRANSPORT INTO THE 21ST CENTURY

While internal air transport throughout the major part of the British Isles has undergone many changes and fundamental rationalisation during the years since the end of the war, the pattern in Scotland has largely remained the same, due to the geography and meteorology of the region. Communities that were remote and isolated a century ago are still remote, and those that were only accessible by oft-treacherous sea-crossing remain so.

The economics of commercial aviation in the United Kingdom remain the same as virtually everywhere in the world – attempting to offer a practical and cost-effective alternative to other means of transport. Commonly this means competing with railways and motorways. Whereas the rest of the UK has undergone a dramatic improvement in road and, despite Dr Beeching's infamous axe, sufficient rail services remain such that, one way or another, few can be considered dependent on air communication, that has not happened in Scotland. In particular the West Coast and Shetlands, have seen not just the need but the necessity of entering into the era of communicational integration, and the demand for the small and regional air services has increased.

While the need can change into a demand through business expansion and medical emergencies, the less straightforward factor has been the mechanism for making such links possible. It is only within the comparative recent times – here considered as the past 65 years – that aircraft, engines, navigational aids and ground-support systems have been available to turn an ideal into reality. Scotland's less-accessible regions have remained that way for reasons that cannot be changed and this means that the operation of normal aircraft is, in the majority of areas, unthinkable.

The STOL aircraft (Short Take-Off and Landing) has evolved greatly since Handley Page perfected the slotted wing and Fowler (and others) showed how to augment lift and control drag using flaps. But none of these would have been of much use without the gas turbine engine offering power (thrust)–to–weight ratios that were unthinkable in the days of the commercial aircraft with the internal combustion engine.

An even greater consideration which has overlaid every aspect of Scottish communications has been the post-war development and expansion of the North Sea oil industry. Unheard of, of course, in pre-war days, nobody could have foreseen just what a major effect this new business would have upon commercial flying, both as regards the development and expansion of existing communications networks as well as the evolution of wholly-new oil industry serving infrastructure epitomised by the growth of off-shore helicopter services. Nowhere else in the British Isles has the impact of a new industry been so great as that of Scotland's North Sea oil involvement. The nearest rival is the arrival of containerisation and the establishment of container ports for shipping but that fresh industry, impressive though it is, impinges in no way on the development of flying services.

The oil industry has transformed Scotland's air traffic pattern. An example of this is to be seen at Kirkwall where this Orcadian airport was discovered and founded at Hatston Farm in 1931. The aerodrome developed as a result of pioneering work by Captain Ernest Edmund 'Ted' Fresson, remained no more than a local halt on the way to Shetland. When oil was exploited in the North Sea, in a matter of months it changed into a busy terminus with heavy daily traffic. In the year 1962-63 for example, Kirkwall saw 1,805 scheduled movements and 38 charters but a decade later (1972-73), while scheduled services had increased by 2.4% to 2,055, charter flights had leapt 56.4% to 3,323 movements.

Helicopter services associated with the industry and its many off-shore oil-rigs have brought a density of traffic, predominantly in the east coast region, that is amongst the highest not just in Great Britain but in the whole of Europe.

Scotland's skies were first challenged in the immediate port-war period by the needs of defence in the Cold War when incursions by Russian aircraft had to be challenged and countered. Commercial needs were in the main served by the use of converted military aircraft – hardly suited to the tiny ill-prepared airstrips still common in the more remote sectors. The fundamental flaw was that no one body (with the noted exception of Scottish Aviation Ltd) possessed sufficient of the overall position to decide how Scottish needs could best be rationalised so as to provide the ideal 'one-size-suits-all' response.

Amidst numerous proposals, the first serious post-war development plan for Scotland's air services did not appear until 1974 with the publication, by the Civil Aviation Authority Study Group, of the report *Air Transport in the Scottish Highlands and Islands.* In 83 closely-printed A4 pages and some 22 additional Appendices, the report concluded that (a) the air transport system in the Scottish Highlands and Islands makes an important contribution to the social and economic well-being of that region and (b) it will ultimately prove impossible to run or otherwise operate such a system without government subsidy for both aerodrome and local air navigation services.

Amongst the Highlands and Islands routes there are indeed several which would not be commercially viable without financial support. Since the mid-1970s, payment of subsidies by the Scottish Government (not, let it be understood, by the British Government) has supported the Glasgow-Tiree and Glasgow-Barra routes. Since most things once happily parochial are now overseen by (and interfered with by) Brussels. European regulations have not overlooked these matters and in the mid-1990s, Public Service Obligations (PSO) were created to regularise the whole subsidy question.

A PSO was defined as an obligation imposed on a carrier to provide a set level of service on a particular route in order to ensure that the service satisfies fixed standards of continuity, regularity, capacity and pricing. The Scottish Executive's take on this was to create a Route Development Fund (RDF) or a subsidy by another name. As a consequence, the effective subsidies have sustained these two routes plus that for Glasgow-Campbeltown through the aegis of a Government contract with Loganair.

PSOs have also been placed on routes within Shetland, Orkney, Comhairle nan Eilean Siar and Argyll and Bute Councils, all of which are subsidised by the local authorities. The subsidy ensures that these isolated communities have air links with a main centre. European Union (*i.e.* Brussels) legislation means that under the terms of the regulation, it is necessary to seek competitive bids on an EU-wide basis to allow subsidy to be paid. This rule consolidates and updates the set of liberalisation measures known as the 'Third Package' adopted in 1992 which defines the economic framework for air transport in the Community. This makes provision for the imposition of PSOs 'for the maintenance of lifeline air services'. It also provides the basis on which non-commercial but economically and socially necessary air services can be subsidised by national or local authorities after the imposition of a PSO to ensure continued operation.

Not that all has worked smoothly in recent years. In 2007 there were grave fears that subsidies for direct flights would be brought to an end as analysts suggested that the Scottish Executive's Route Development Fund (RDF) would become 'unworkable' following revised EU regulations to be applied that June in spite of considerable lobbying from Scotland and elsewhere.

In the event, while subsidies for new routes were made considerably more difficult to obtain, the RDF system, in a different form, survives. Scotland's position to fighting this corner has been soundly based on the premise that some of the flights subsidised are to destinations in the UK where there are no obvious rail or road alternatives. Regional and internal air transport in the 21st century is unquestionably not as straightforward as it was 50 years ago but, as we are oft reminded as an excuse for anything that makes us worse off than we were before, that's progress. As it stands the Scottish Government still subsidises essential flights to the remoter areas of the Highlands and Islands through its Air Discount Scheme.

After a battle to achieve EU approval, it is agreed that anybody living in Colonsay, Islay, Jura, Orkney, Shetland, the Western Isles or, on the mainland, Caithness and North West Sutherland can apply for membership to the Air Discount Scheme. As members they will obtain a 40% discount on the flight ticket price for flights within the defined region and to Scottish hub airports. The Scottish Government will pay the airline the residual cost of the ticket. For some, though, this is not enough as business interests continue to highlight the need to offer support to long distance flights that can bring more business into Scotland. But this is now a political hot potato...

Not exactly made in Scotland but certainly paid for by the Scots! One of the most common fighter aircraft of the First World War was the Sopwith 1F1 Camel and this one, E7223, was sponsored by the Kincardineshire Parish of Banchory Ternan. The aircraft was built by steam traction engine makers Ruston, Proctor & Co of Lincoln. This firm made some 2,750 aircraft between 1914 and 1918 as well as 3,000 engines – it was the largest UK supplier. And this Camel was just one of 1,600 the firm constructed. During both wars, towns and villages were invited to 'buy' an aircraft via a public collection. During the Second World War it was often the incentive of a row of pennies along the High Street which remarkably soon could tally for a Spitfire or a Hurricane. *Picture from the collection of Richard Stenlake.*

AIRCRAFT BUILT AND FLOWN IN SCOTLAND

Throughout the First World War, many military aircraft were manufactured in Scotland for the defence of the British Isles. The main companies involved included Arrol-Johnston Ltd (Heathhall, Dumfries); Barclay Curle Ltd (Whiteinch); William Beardmore Ltd (Dalmuir); British Caudron Co (Bowhouse Farm, Alloa); William Denny & Brothers (Dumbarton); Fairfield Engineering Co (Govan); Henderson Scottish Aviation Factory (Grieg & Henderson, Aberdeen); Napier & Miller Ltd (Old Kilpatrick); Alexander Stephen & Sons (Linthouse, Govan); G & J Weir Ltd (Cathcart, Renfrewshire). There were, however, others the names of which are now lost. It is known that aircraft emerged from some unlikely locations as demand accelerated. The Glasgow Corporation Tram Depot at Coplawhill was one of these.

Aircraft produced included large runs of Sopwith Camels, BE.2e and BE.2c, Sopwith Snipes, Fairey Campania Flying Boats, Sopwith Pups, Avro 504K, Airco DH.9, Wight Flying Boat, Handley Page V/1500 giant bombers, and many others. Virtually every type of front-line aircraft was produced in Scottish factories – not to mention airships and balloons, a Beardmore speciality. Aircraft engines were also built by Beardmore (which had secured the Austro-Daimler manufacturing licence) and BHP (Beardmore, Halford and Pullinger), while, later, other motors were built or assembled.

A project that never reached fruition was the enthusiastically-promoted manufacture of the 'all-metal British Burnelli Mk.II', a twin-Kestrel-powered 14-passenger aircraft built along the 'flying wing' idea of American engineer Vincent Justus Burnelli. In November 1936 a company called Scottish Aircraft & Engineering Co Ltd announced the early opening of a factory on the Clyde to build the 'Clyde Clipper' as it was dubbed. The plans, backed by British American Tobacco Ltd's chairman Sir Hugo Cunliffe-Owen (1870-1947) and promoted by the Aviation Committee of the Scottish Development Council, collapsed in acrimonious disarray and a Receiver was appointed on July 26th, 1937.

By the time of the Second World War, aircraft manufacture was far more fragmented than in the Great War as the importance of decentralization of factories became of paramount importance. In that conflict, component production thus dominated where complete aircraft had once been the goal.

BEARDMORE

During the war, many BE.2c aircraft and Sopwith Pups had been built by this old-established firm. The company identified that there was a naval application for the aircraft but that it needed to be smaller for storage. The firm came up with its first 'own design' peacetime aircraft which it called the WB.III. Based very much on the Pup it had folding wings. Trials proved that the Beardmore modifications and 'improvements' actually interfered with the aircrafts otherwise ideal handling conditions. A few were delivered to the Admiralty but no great orders were forthcoming. The company went on to design and build several others – the WB.IV and V – but they failed to achieve success.

The largest wartime aircraft built by the firm were the giant Handley Page four-engined V/1500 bombers. Too large to be flown from Dalmuir, they had to be taken by road to Inchinnan near Erskine in Renfrew, and reassembled for flight.

The company also built airships, the most successful of which was probably the R34 launched in March 1919 at a cost of some £350,000. Trials began on March 14th, 1919, at Inchinnan between Renfrew and Greenock. Delivered to the RAF at East Fortune, R34 then flew to the United States carrying 6,000 gallons of petrol for the trip. Setting off just after midnight on July 2nd 1919, the flight was uncomfortable and comfort was a weighty commodity intentionally left behind. At nine in the morning on July 6th, R34 was overhead Hazlehurst Field, Mineola, New York. The Scottish airship had made it! There were 140 gallons of petrol left in the tanks. Three days later, with a strong tailwind, she made the return trip, taking 75 hours and three minutes at an average speed of 51 mph. The total of 7,420 miles had been accomplished at about 43 mph.

William Beardmore & Company of Inchinnan built several airships for the British Admiralty beginning with the '24' – a designation before the use of a prefacing capital letter. The 24 was a Vickers design and flew a total of 164 hours 12 minutes. Next came an 'all-Beardmore design', the R27, a triple-engined craft of the so-called 23X Class evolved by Vickers. This notched up 849 hours 40 minutes of flight time before being destroyed by fire at Howden on August 16th, 1918. By far the best-known was R34 which cost £350,000 to build and achieved more than 500 hours in the air. In July 1919 it crossed the Atlantic to New York where it moored at Roosevelt Field, Long Island.

Top: The officers and crew of the R34.

Centre: The R34 taking on supplies at East Fortune in preparation for its Atlantic flight.

Bottom: This US Navy photograph shows the centre, parallel portion of the airship. In the foreground are stacks of bottle of hydrogen needed to replenish the airship's supply for the return trip.

Having flown around 400 hours, R34 suffered a mishap during a trip to her new home at Howden, East Yorkshire. In darkness and poor weather, she flew into a hill and was damaged beyond repair. Beardmore's next and last airship was the R36, larger and better than the R34. But after just 80 hours flying, the large and unwieldy vehicle was blown into its own hangar doors during efforts to house her. That Dalmuir sausage never flew again.

For the 1924 Light Aeroplane Contest held at Lympne in Kent, Beardmore entered an extraordinary ultra light monoplane powered by a Bristol Cherub flat twin engine of 30 hp. This little all-wood aeroplane managed to score the highest marks in most of the categories and consequently won the Air Ministry prize of £2,000. An excellent fillip for the firm but hardly a financial success for there proved to be no market for so underpowered a light plane. It did, though, make history.

For some reason, William Beardmore & Company now fell under the spell of a famed German designer, Dr-Ing Adolf Rohrbach, formerly of Zeppelin-Staaken, who had set up Rohrbach Metall-Flugzeugbau in Berlin in 1922 to design and build large all-metal monoplanes with stressed skin structures, unusual for the time. Because of the provisions of the Treaty of Versailles which restricted Germany's aircraft industry, Rohrbach formed a subsidiary firm in Denmark to assemble aircraft. Beardmore, seeing a great opportunity (which was actually never there), became a Rohrbach licensee and visualised producing a load of Rohrbachs at Dalmuir.

Rohrbach's portfolio included a whole range of land- and waterplanes. For its first efforts, Beardmore settled on the Rohrbach Ro VI, a three-engined bomber aircraft. Conforming to principles supplied by Rohrbach for the Ro VI, the Beardmore company designed what was for its time a massive all-metal three-engined transport to which it gave the name *Inflexible*. Not without just cause would the firm promote it as 'the World's Largest Monoplane' when it eventually lumbered into the air. The aircraft, serial number J7557, was built in sections at Dalmuir between 1925 and 1927 and these were sent by sea to Felixstowe and from there delivered by road to the Aeroplane Armament Experimental Establishment (A&AEE) at Martlesham Heath, six miles east of Ipswich in Suffolk. Here it was assembled and first flown on March 5th, 1928. It took part in the RAF Hendon Air Display that summer having also been the unlikely star of the Norwich Aero Club annual flying display.

Structurally advanced for its time, the *Inflexible* possessed reasonably good flying characteristics. Of very large proportions, the wing span was 157 feet 6 inches but at an all-up weight of 37,000 lbs, it was grossly underpowered with its three 650 hp Rolls-Royce Condor II engines.

The *Inflexible* was impressive for its size but did not garner any official interest or production. Dismantled at Martlesham Heath in 1930, the component parts were used to investigate the effects of corrosion on light-alloy stressed skin structures. London's Science Museum collection preserves one of the seven-foot diameter wheels.

Beardmore's second application of the Rohrbach design licence was what was called the Beardmore BeRo.2 Inverness flying boat which, like the *Inflexible*, was an all-metal monoplane aimed at the RAF. Two examples were ordered, N183 and N184. The first was built by Rohrbach's Danish subsidiary and the second was assembled at Dalmuir. The Danish example was the first to be completed and arrived with the Marine Aircraft Experimental Establishment at Felixstowe on September 18th, 1925. Initial trials showed the aircraft possessed unacceptable handling qualities both in the air and on the water and had a poor performance. It was damaged beyond economic repair during strength testing in May 1927.

The Dalmuir example incorporated a revised fuel and cooling system and a servo tab to the rudder. Powered by Napier Lion engines, the two engines were pylon-mounted above the wing centre-section rather like the Saro Cutty Sark amphibians. Like the Inflexible, the aircraft was ugly in the extreme and, although being primarily made of duralumin and having a 'cantilever' wing, as before shallow lift wires braced mainplane to fuselage. A crew of four was carried. By far the oddest feature was the provision of a folding mast and sails so that in the event of engine malfunction or fuel deprivation, the aircraft could be 'converted' into a sailing boat.

Transported to the sheltered waters of the Gare Loch, and launched at Roseneath (today Rosneath), it made its maiden flight on November 30th, 1928, and, like its Danish-built predecessor, revealed both poor handling and performance. The programme was stopped in April 1929 and N184 was scrapped.

Besides the ultra-light Wee Bee, Beardmore did not enjoy much success in the first decade after the end of the war. It had also operated a flying school but everything came to an end in 1929 when the Air Ministry declined to continue financing its operation. In February Dalmuir closed down its aircraft division. Eight months later the Stock Market Crash forced other companies to shut up shop. While Beardmore-made aircraft were now old history, Beardmore staff went on to better things and in particular Helmuth John Stieger, a Beardmore designer, and test pilot Rolo de Haga Haig went on to form the Monospar Aircraft Company, forerunner of General Aircraft Ltd.

BLACKBURN

With the encouragement of Sir Maurice Denny of the shipbuilders Denny Brothers, Robert Blackburn of the Blackburn Aircraft Company Ltd of Brough was encouraged to set up a factory on the Clyde at Dumbarton to produce aircraft. This old-established Yorkshire-based aircraft manufacturer opened its Scottish division in 1937 and, with the coming of war, was soon in sub-contract work. Among the types built or assembled at Dumbarton were the Blackburn Shark, Blackburn Botha, Blackburn B20 and B40 prototypes, Short Sunderland. Major production runs were for the Botha (200 completed) and the Sunderland (260 completed). The last Sunderland came off the production line on October 25th, 1945. Later the plant produced components for the Blackburn Firebrand and the Buccaneer and, after the merger with General Aircraft Ltd, components for the General Aircraft Universal which was re-named the Blackburn & General Beverley. The factory closed in 1961.

Kay's Gyroplane represented an independent development that was not associated with Cierva, although Cierva and David Kay are reported to have met and exchanged ideas. Kay originated his own rotor design from first principles and G-ACVA was sufficiently different from that of Cierva as to be free of design infringement. It had collective pitch control and the rotor head could be tilted from side to side for lateral control while a conventional tail provided rudder and elevators. After that February 1935 first flight Kay tried to get some official interest in his machine. As a result, that September the machine went to RAE Farnborough and began six months of extensive tests. The outcome was satisfactory but encouragement stopped far short of what David Kay hoped for. Jump-start was a novel feature of the little Kay single-seater Gyroplane and it was reputed to have the ability to leap to between ten and twenty feet vertically.

DAVID KAY AND HIS GYROPLANES

David Kay of Blackford, Perth, was an autogyro genius who, operating quite independently of the Spaniard Juan de la Cierva, began work in the late 1920s on his wholly-original form of autogyro which he would term his Gyroplane.

It must be pointed out here that Cierva patented the name 'Autogiro' (spelled with a capital initial letter and a letter 'i' in the second syllable) as the name of his invention. The generic term, though, is 'autogyro'.

With the assistance of John Grieve of Scone and using models to evaluate a system of rotor control that he had devised, he designed the first Kay Gyroplane and had it built by Shields Garage in Perth. Kay was thus Great Britain's autogyro pioneer. The two machines that Kay was ultimately to design each had four-blade rotors and were single-seaters that differed from the contemporary Cierva designs in having no 'wings' or aileron-carrying spars.

The first prototype (which never bore a civil registration) was built in an *ad hoc* manner by a local garage and fitted with wire-spoked motorcycle wheels, but the second, G-ACVA, was contracted out to Oddie, Bradbury & Cull Ltd at Eastleigh Airport, Southampton. This company had considerable expertise in autogiro work and also made parts for the newly-formed Cierva Autogiro Company Ltd at Hanworth.

Kay's crucial invention was the control of flight by altering the angles of incidence of the rotor blades. This fundamental difference from the then-current thinking of Cierva allowed the incidence of the blades to be adjusted at will during flight. Kay was granted a patent for this which clearly describes the first-ever application of collective pitch control in conjunction with a sideways tilting rotor.

Another pioneering device was a facility for spinning the rotor up to speed from the engine, allowing a very short take-off run. Kay had several meetings with Cierva including one significant one on April 27th 1927 when he proposed collaboration based on his Patent that would result in an autogiro with a collective pitch-based control system, a sideways tilting rotor and other improvements. Cierva, however, was not receptive to such ideas, believing that the solution to any problem lay in avoiding all complications to the simple rotor system that he had tried and tested.

Both of Kay's Gyroplanes were the subject of extensive tests by Air Ministry officials at RAF Leuchars in Fife during 1932 and, three years later, by the Royal Aircraft Establishment (RAE) at Farnborough. David Kay formed Kay Gyroplanes Ltd, registered in Edinburgh in November 1933 at 18, Atholl Crescent, with fellow directors James S Hogg, James McLaren Taylor and Lieutenant Colonel Maurice Ormonde Darby who had been associated with the Aircraft Disposal Company Ltd at Croydon Airport. Several British patents were taken out in the names of David Kay and John William Dyer.

In the end, insufficient funds prevented further development of the Gyroplane but in August of 1937 a newly-formed business, Scottish Aircraft Construction Company, was founded by Alan Muntz of Heston Aerodrome which paid Kay a reputed £70,000, £10,000 of which was in cash, for the design and all rights to the aircraft. It was stated that the business had the backing of Lord Weir of the Weir Autogiro business in Cathcart who was also a senior director of Cierva, and that the intention was to manufacture the Gyroplane in quantity. It never came to pass. In its time, the Kay Gyroplane was both the fastest and smallest autogiro in the country. David Kay remains one of the forgotten geniuses of the British autogiro scene.

An interesting, unsubstantiated, tale published by the Blackford Historical Society (2013), relates how during the war, David Kay was sent to Canada as a flying instructor, returning to train pilots at Scone. During the time, the story suggests, the 'patent ran out during his call up to [the] RAF and was taken up by others'. American servicemen were posted to Britain and one apparently related the story how 'Lt Sikorsky persuaded David Kay's brother Andrew to show him the autogyro *[sic]* plans which he then copied and produced and patented the Sikorsky helicopter'.

Prestwick-built SA Bulldog T.1 XX671 was one of a batch of 130 constructed for the Royal Air Force. A large number of bulldogs went to the Swedish Air Force as well and these all were allocated British civil registrations for the ferry flights across the North Sea.

SCOTTISH AVIATION BULLDOG

The Beagle Aircraft Company at Shoreham in Sussex was a Government-funded company created originally out of a merger of F G Miles Aircraft Ltd, Auster Aircraft Ltd, Wallis Autogyros, and backed by the Pressed Steel Company. Founded in October 1960, it produced a number of good general aviation and light aircraft, among these the Pup and the larger Bulldog which was intended as a military trainer and first flew at Shoreham on May 19th, 19169. However, through over-optimism, bad management and ineptitude, the company entered financial problems from which recovery was impossible. The firm was wound up in January 1970. It did, however, possess a useful order book including a large and unfulfilled order for Bulldogs from the Swedish Air Force.

Scottish Aviation Ltd subsequently took over Bulldog production, shifted the entire enterprise to Prestwick and honoured outstanding contracts while achieving new orders from the RAF. Re-named the Scottish Aviation Bulldog, it was an all-metal two-seat side-by-side (with optional third seat) training aircraft powered by a Rolls-Royce built Continental engine. The Swedish order for 78 machines was duly delivered in 1971. In the end, the largest customer was the Royal Air Force, which placed an order for 130 Bulldogs in 1972, entering service as the Bulldog T.1. It was used extensively as a basic trainer, in particular as the standard aircraft of the University Air Squadrons and, later, Air Experience Flights, providing flying training. Later examples were known as British Aerospace Bulldogs after Scottish Aviation Ltd was absorbed into that conglomerate.

By the early 2000s, the RAF had replaced the Bulldog as a trainer by the Grob Tutor and the Bulldogs were disposed of to an enthusiastic private-ownership market which was appreciative of the aircraft's excellent visibility, robustness and aerobatic capability.

On January 1st, 1969, St Andrews University Air Squadron merged with its counterpart at Edinburgh to form ELUAS or East Lowlands Universities Air Squadron. Edinburgh UAS was formed in 1941 and St Andrews the following year with flying based on RAF Turnhouse and RAF Leuchars respectively. In those times the mainstay was the de Havilland Tiger Moth but early in the 1950s they were replaced by the DHC Chipmunk T.10. ELUAS took over the initial flying training of all the students of the universities that were previously served by the two individual partners and in 1969 Edinburgh's Heriot-Watt University was added followed, in 1974, by Stirling. Three years later Napier University (then called Napier College of Commerce & Technology) was added. In 1975 the Chipmunks were retired and replaced by the SAL Bulldog. In a move to improve accessibility, St Andrews departed in 1981 to join with Aberdeen and Dundee UASs to found the stupendously cumbersome ADStAUAS (you work it out) at RAF Leuchars. In the way of things, this parting of the two was ultimately resolved for, with RAF Turnhouse facing closure, ELUAS re-located to Leuchars in 1996. Here we see XX524 setting off from its base at Turnhouse for a flight on April 9th 1992. The tiny white thing on the hangar door behind the aircraft's tail is a winding handle by means of which the huge steel hangar doors can be opened – a modern replacement for the time-honoured ten airmen and a call of 'Two-Six!' After a quarter of a century of service, the Bulldogs were replaced by the German-built Grob 115E which the RAF styled the Tutor T1.

Scottish Aviation's Prestwick Pioneer was a remarkable STOL aircraft which, in pre-war days, would have stolen the American Guggenheim Prize without contest. Designed to meet a military specification for an ultra-slow-landing aircraft that could operate from unprepared ground, the four-seater (pilot and three passengers) was a stunning design by New Zealand-born Robert McIntyre who, despite sharing the same name, was no relation to Wing Commander David Fowler McIntyre, founder and owner of Scottish Aviation Ltd. With its extensive full-span leading-edge slats and vast barn-door Fowler flaps, the 5,800-lb aircraft could fly under full control below 35 mph and land in little more than 100 feet. And once, in conditions of snow, the measured landing run was 26 yards! The prototype was fitted with a 240 hp DH Gipsy Queen 32 but production models (styled the Pioneer 2) had either 520 hp Avis Leonides radials or the 560 hp variant. This one, G-AOGK, first flew on January 29th 1956, got its C of A on February 1st and then went to No.78 Squadron, Aden, as XL517. Notice the long stirrup on the port side to help the pilot mount his charge – necessary because of the high-energy, tall undercarriage. At extreme angles of attack with the nose held high for maximum lift and low forward speed, it was necessary for the tailplane to pivot between +4deg and -9deg, a range of movement controlled by an electrically-driven screw jack.

SCOTTISH AVIATION PRESTWICK PIONEER

With a crew of one and the ability to carry four passengers, the single-engined Prestwick Pioneer was a most remarkable aircraft. Designer of the machine was New Zealand-born Robert McIntyre (no relation to David F McIntyre), and his brief was to make an aircraft that would fulfil an army-co-operation role for mixed and varied duties including casualty evacuation. First flown on November 5th, 1947, and aimed at short-field performance from unprepared landing strips, it was one of the earliest post-war STOL (Short Take-Off and Landing) aircraft. Initially it was fitted with a 240 hp Gipsy Queen inline engine. However, the performance was disappointing and so the Alvis Leonides engine which, at 520 hp, was more than double that of the original, was fitted and with this the machine was able to demonstrate fully its remarkable flight envelope. While 53 aircraft were used by the RAF, examples were also used by the Malay and Ceylonese air forces. The machine came into its own during the Malaysian Emergency and served in Aden and Cyprus.

Phil Burton was flight commander on 209 Squadron and then 20 Squadron at Seletar and then Tengah during 1967-69. Of the Pioneer he wrote:

> It was the best flying I ever did and I grew to respect this tough aircraft and its abilities whether it was landing on carriers or on the interesting 'one way in' strips. Our most interesting trips were with Special Forces and the mission that we maintained in Laos. Everybody shot at us, including the Royal Thai Air Force. We ended up flying either over 3500 ft or very low - well under 50 feet. Night approaches into remote strips were also an event to be remembered. We had a lot of crunches, but no fatalities. On the short take off, I once annoyed ATC at Tengah after being asked to take off immediately and took off from the holding point: they weren't amused. We could do backwards circuits at Seletar by getting airborne, climbing then slowing down to drift slowly backwards if the breeze was strong enough, then accelerating in the descent back on to the runway: at night that was a real laugh....

The life of these aircraft was remarkably hard and many landings were best described as 'controlled crashes'. That the aircraft survived so long is a lasting credit to the Prestwick team.

The second of Robert McIntyre's designs for Scottish Aviation Ltd was the 16-seat Twin Pioneer which used as outer wing panels the wings of the Prestwick Pioneer. It was powered by two Alvis Leonides engines of power ranging from 540 in the prototype to 640 hp in the Series III. Like its predecessor, the 'Twin-Pin' as it was affectionately known had a phenomenal STOL performance and was quickly identified as ideal for use in jungle and tropical air-strips. The third machine built was G-AOEO seen here on climb-out. This particular example embarked on a sales and demonstration tour of the Middle East. Meanwhile, a fatal accident to another aircraft had revealed a weakness in the lower attachment point of the lift struts. All aircraft were undergoing modifications to the new standard but SAL's founder and managing director, D F McIntyre was not open to being delayed and went ahead with the tour before this aircraft was modified. On December 8th, 1957, the port wing came off in flight and McIntyre, his pilot Captain Roy Smith and the company's engineering officer R C Clapham all lost their lives.

SCOTTISH AVIATION TWIN PIONEER

From the Pioneer, it was a short step to produce a twin-engined variant that could operate as a STOL transport/airliner. In this aircraft, the Pioneer's wings would be used complete with slots slats and flap, as the outer panels to a new centre-section. The prototype, fitted with a pair of Alvis Leonides radials, first flew on June 25th, 1955 and would be the first of some 87 examples made before production ceased in 1960. The company laid on plans to produce 200 aircraft but during field trials of the second pre-production Twin Pioneer in Tripoli, Libya, structural failure occurred at a known weak-spot on one lift strut attachment point. Scottish Aviation's co-founder David McIntyre, the pilot and the company engineering officer all lost their lives. Ironically, this weakness had been detected following an earlier accident and all aircraft were being modified: McIntyre did not want to delay his demonstration schedule and did not wait for the mod to be carried out on this machine. The company and the project survived this tragedy and the aircraft served the RAF in Malaysia and Nepal. The Series 2 and 3 models were fitted with larger engines, the latter with 640 hp Leonides while the Series 2 had 600 hp Pratt & Whitney Wasp single row radials. Later a number of surplus aircraft were civilianised for use by small charter airlines and other private use.

SCOTTISH AVIATION JETSTREAM

Designed by Charles Frederick Joy, the Handley Page Jetstream was first announced in January 1966. A twin-turboprop executive and feeder-line transport, the aircraft had a pressurised cabin and was aimed at the US market. It carried a crew of two plus stewardess and accommodation for between four and eighteen passengers according to specification. It was also said that the first batch of twenty aircraft had been pre-ordered by the American agent. The prototype first flew on August 18th, 1967. To speed up production, the Radlett-based company negotiated sub-contract production with SAL for the manufacture of the wings at Prestwick as a result of which SAL made a heavy investment in jigs, tools and equipment.

Handley Page had been experiencing its own problems with the withdrawal of military contracts and consequently placed considerable reliance on the Jetstream. It all proved too little too late and the famous old company went into voluntary liquidation in March 1970 being wound up after 61 years of existence. This left Scottish Aviation Ltd in a dilemma for its project investment had been considerable. The decision was taken to take the ultimate step and acquire the entire project from the liquidators. SAL continued production and development under a consortium called Jetstream Aircraft.

When SAL was merged into British Aerospace in 1977, further development work continued and there have been various new models produced including examples for the RAF. The aircraft now became the BAe Jetstream. This was the last machine to be produced at Prestwick and, in May, 1997, BAe announced the closure of the Jetstream 41 production line. The last aircraft came off the assembly line in 1998 marking the end of over half a century of Prestwick-based aircraft production.

Besides this work, throughout its existence Scottish Aviation had carried out a great deal of contract manufacture, rebuilding and conversion work. During the early part of the war it manufactured de Havilland DH.82B Queen Bee radio-controlled target aircraft. Of the total of 380 examples made, Scottish Aviation Ltd made 60 in a factory at 39 West Campbell Street, Glasgow. Although similar in appearance to the Tiger Moth, these aircraft used the all-wood fuselage of the DH.60GIII Moth Major and were powered by a Gipsy Major I engine. Post-war civilian work involved conversions starting with producing passenger transports from military aircraft in 1946 (notably DC-3 aircraft into BEA 'Pionair' airliners). In the mid-1960s it initiated a freighter conversion for the Vickers Viscount. Known as the Viscount 808, three aircraft were modified to combined freighter/passenger configuration for Aer Lingus. The first was G-BBDK converted in 1967.

The Jetstream became a saviour of Scottish Aviation Ltd and in 1972 the Government awarded the company an order for 26 aircraft, later increased to 28. Eventually, after SAL was absorbed by British Aerospace, it became known as the BAe Jetstream 31 but was still produced in what had been the SAL factory at Prestwick. The Jetstream was a world wide success story and across the years some 490 airframes would be built at Prestwick. The original makers, Handley Page, clearly had had a winner on their hands when lack of funds forced liquidation. Here are two early models flying in the United States of America. United Airlines used these on West Coast routes while Presidential Airways employed them in the Eastern USA. More than 170 were ordered for the North American market.

James G Weir was head of the company G & J Weir which was involved in marine pumps and boilers. However he was also interested in aeronautics and, having observed Juan de la Cierva's demonstration of his Autogiro at Farnborough in 1925, he and the financier Hugh Kindersley played a major part in the formation of the Cierva Autogiro Company Ltd. From that time forward, Weir played a major part in the research and development work on Autogiros. Weir had a licence to build its own autogiros and it made three variants before seeing the advantages of the helicopter moved its resources in that direction. The giant Cierva Air Horse was the culmination of the development work undertaken by Weir remembering that Juan de la Cierva had been killed in an airliner accident in December 1936. When the Air Horse was lost in 1950 and the British authorities were looking to America for helicopter technology, James Weir protested that we had the technology and Britain should support its own industry in rotary wing development. Of course, it didn't happen and Glasgow's pioneering spirit that drove James Weir was crushed. Weir's first autogiro had flown in the closing months of 1932 and it was called the W-1. His second was the W-2 pictured here at Hanworth, home of the Cierva company. Built at Cathcart it was powered by a specially-built flat twin engine called the Douglas Dryad which featured a reduction gear drive to the propeller and produced between 45 and 50 hp. The W-2 was a small single-seater and a very good flyer.

THE WEIR AUTOGIROS

The engineering company of G & J Weir Ltd at Cathcart, Glasgow, was founded in 1871 by Airdrie-born James (1842-July 10th 1920) and George Weir. At the age of 23, George went to sea as a marine engineer before starting his business first in Liverpool. Two years later he returned to Glasgow where he made many improvements to the marine boiler. In 1887 he opened a foundry for the manufacture of his inventions which included pumps. This plant ultimately expanded to thirteen acres in area and employed a workforce close to 1,500 strong.

Among the innovations he introduced was the use of electricity as a motive power instead of steam and he was an early advocate of the bonus scheme where a worker's diligence and dexterity was reflected in his pay-packet. James Weir had two sons, William Douglas Weir (1877-1959) who was to become Viscount Weir of Eastwood, and James George Weir (1887-1973). The latter learned to fly at Hendon on a Blériot Monoplane during 1910 gaining Aviators' Certificate No.24 dated November 8th 1910. He enjoyed a distinguished career in the Royal Flying Corps quickly attaining the rank of air commodore.

In 1902, Sir William Douglas Weir took over as managing director of the family business and, in 1912, became its chairman. During the First World War, Weir produced shells for the bombs and on July 24th 1915 Sir William Weir resigned as managing director to join the Ministry of Munitions with responsibility for the West of Scotland. His factory turned to aircraft manufacture in 1917. By the end of the conflict G & J Weir had assembled 1,427 aircraft. Weir became Secretary of State for the Royal Air Force, and received a knighthood in 1917 and in 1918 was elevated to the peerage as Lord Weir. At the end of the war he returned to direct G & J Weir Ltd. and during the 1920s succeeded in surviving an industrial slump. One of Lord

Weir's major achievements was to secure a continued, independent existence for the RAF in 1923. Another of his achievements was to chair a committee, which saw the establishment of the national electricity grid.

The younger son of George Weir, James George Weir, became chairman of Cierva Autogiro Co and at the same time headed up a small design team at Cathcart to develop a range of autogiros with the backing of Cierva. Additionally, the availability of a company-owned foundry inspired the design and construction of an engine and this, named the Weir Pixie, would power one of their machines.

Joined by two designers, James Allan Jamieson Bennett (who was already with Weirs on a part-time basis as a physicist) and Cyril George Pullin who later took charge of the aircraft department. Weir's first Autogiro was designated the Cierva C.28 but it became known as the W-1 which was first flown by Cierva himself. The W-2 was similar but with improved rotor drive and control system. The further improved W-3 (with an engine designed by Pullin and former Douglas engine designer Michael Walker) progressed to the W-4 which was the last Autogiro Weir produced for with the virtual departure of Bennett to run Cierva after the death of the Spaniard, Pullin and Weir decided to move into helicopters, the W-5 and the W-6 being the last completed before the outbreak of war. In 1943, Cierva merged with Weir to form Cierva Rotorcraft.

HOME-BUILT LIGHT AIRCRAFT

The thriving home-built aircraft movement in post-war years has not left Scotland untouched and since the 1950s there have been numerous amateur aircraft registered. Several Druine D.31 Turbulents and two-seat D.53 Turbi aircraft, a number of Luton LA.4a Minors and at least three Luton LA.5A Majors have been built, the best known of which is probably Minor G-AXGR built at Longniddry, East Lothian by the father and son R and W Spall. Rutherglen's Turbi first flew from Strathaven as far back as July 1960.

Autogyros have not been overlooked and the Montgomerie Merlin, a much-modified version of the Bensen BM-8 design was designed and built in 1992 by J M Montgomerie of Kirkmichael Road, Crosshill, Maybole, Ayrshire. The aircraft has since evolved and its designer has sold sets of plans to other enthusiasts.

Private aircraft ownership was rife in the 1930s and its spread through Scotland was no exception. One of the more interesting types in the hands of the enthusiast flyer was this German-built Klemm L-25-1A, imported and first registered in Britain on June 16th 1930. Just before war broke out it was acquired by Robert H Grant of Dumfries who wisely put it into storage 'for the duration'. It was registered to him on November 11th 1946 but it would be more than another decade before its first post-war C of A would be issued. It had the misfortune to have its hangar collapse upon it but is, reputedly, still extant and awaiting the next enthusiastic pair of hands.

PRIVATE FLYING AND THE FLYING CLUBS

The term 'private flying' was created after the end of the First World War. Prior to that, there was effectively no such thing. The first private person to own an aircraft in Scotland was James George Weir (1887-1973) who acquired his Boulton & Paul P.9 two-seat wooden biplane G-EASJ on July 15th, 1920. He kept it at Renfrew. Private aviation came with a vengeance when, in September 1922 the first King's Cup Race took place and included a stop at Renfrew. The first competitor to arrive was Captain Franklin Leslie Barnard (1896-1927) in AirCo DH.4a G-EAMU *City of York.*

With the Government's decision to assist in founding a number of flying clubs across the British Isles, the foundation of the Glasgow Light Aeroplane Club was announced in 1924. However for various reasons it did not qualify for an Air Ministry subsidy and seems to have disappeared. However, after several false starts, a proper club was successfully inaugurated three years later.

Claimed to be the oldest of the Scottish clubs, the Scottish Aero Club was founded at Glasgow's Renfrew Aerodrome in 1927 with Lord Weir of Eastwood as first president. With four DH Gipsy III Moth aircraft plus two Hornet Moths and a Leopard Moth, the club soon registered a 500-strong membership. That October, Secretary of State for Air Sir Samuel Hoare announced a three-year subsidy scheme which granted flying clubs £50 for every 'A' Licence gained in club flying with a further £10 for the annual renewal of each licence attained within the scheme. There was also an allowance of 30/- per hour flown by each club member up to a maximum of twenty hours. The total grant to each club in the scheme was limited to £2,000 per annum.

The Scottish Flying Club was enrolled into the scheme. The General Council of Light Aeroplane Clubs had, at that time, registered fourteen clubs across the country as members. It was a popular subsidy that resulted in a rapid rise in club membership. The impending start of scheduled air services into Renfrew marked the writing on the wall for the Scottish Flying Club and so, in 1956, it merged with the Strathlay Flying Club to form the Scottish Aero Club and moved to Scone, better known as Perth Aerodrome.

Besides the established aerodromes, there were any number of private landing strips and Gillies relates that around Glasgow alone there were private fields at Newton Mearns, Bridge of Weir, Clarkston, Burnside, Coatbridge, Kilsyth, Bishopbriggs and Lanark. In Ayrshire, at least ten fields were known to be used for private flying while in the Borders, a dozen were recorded. The true number of these unestablished fields can never be known.

GLIDING AND SOARING

Gliding goes back to the days of the unhappy Mr Pilcher but then experienced something of a low point for three and more decades. While gliding had a post-First World War revival with the *Daily Mail*-sponsored trials at Itford Hill in distant East Sussex in October of 1922, nothing of any significance took place in Scotland until the nationwide resurgence in gliding that began later that decade.

The catalyst came with the formation of The British Gliding Association at the end of 1929 which sparked off a steady stream of gliding clubs across the British Isles. The formation of the major English gliding clubs that followed was marked by the appearance on September 6th 1930, of a brand new weekly magazine called *The Sailplane and Glider* edited voluntarily by a staff member of the magazine *The Aeroplane*, 25-year-old Thurstan James. James laboured long and hard to encourage the gliding movement to gather its own momentum. That he succeeded was much to his personal enthusiasm. In 1932 the magazine became the official organ of the British Gliding Association and a new editor, Frank Entwistle, took command. One year later he was replaced by Alan Slater who would remain at the helm well into modern times.

Scotland was not slow in adopting gliding almost as a national sport and the autumn of 1930 saw the founding of a number of clubs, amongst these early examples being The Scottish Flying Club at Renfrew, the Falkirk & District Aviation Club at Westerglen (which was allowed to hold its Monday night meetings in the welfare canteen of the Falkirk Iron Works), and The Glasgow Gliding Club which met at the St

The gliding movement, although representing the oldest and original form of heavier-than-air flight as practised by Percy Pilcher and revived by the British Gliding Competitions staged at Itford on England's South Downs in 1922, did not really come into its own until the end of the 1920s and early 1930s. In those early days, gliding was just that. You went up having been pulled into the air by a bunch of helpers using an elastic cord or by a fixed rope and a motor-car – and you came down again. Soaring, pioneered by the Germans, required more expensive gliders. To begin with people learned on very basic gliders like this one. The Germans had made a very simple glider comprising an 'A'-frame, tail and wings and called it the Zögling (pupil). The style was quickly copied in the Dickson glider made by Southampton-based Cloudcraft and then the Guildford firm of RFD run by Reginald Foster Dagnall produced their own 'pupil' teacher naturally called the Dagling! One of Scotland's oldest clubs was the Glasgow Gliding Club which met at Barrance Farm, Easter Whitecraigs.

Andrews Halls in Berkeley Street. This club, inaugurated in June 1930, flew from Barrance Farm at Easter Whitecraigs every Sunday and received enthusiastic if sometimes over-the-top support from *The Daily Record and Mail* which ran a weekly column of 'gliding notes'. Edinburgh Gliding Club also flew every Sunday from West Craigs Farm between Corstorphine and Turnhouse Aerodrome.

The Falkirk club, like almost every other gliding club, was dependent on friendly farmers who would allow them to 'borrow' a bit of land. Arrangements at Westerglen terminated in December 1930 and it was not until the end of January 1931 that Mr Reid of Glen Farm in Glen village, came to their rescue. The only problem was that the new field had a pronounced slope and was partially obstructed by a canal, a railway track and some high tension cables. That the club was able to fly illustrates the tenacity of the members who were keen to fly.

An unusual series of events staged in the summer of 1931 were the demonstrations of soaring flights sponsored by the British Gliding Association in conjunction with Lyons Tea. On May 30th – 31st, Glasgow's Campsie Fells was the site of one of these displays. The length of the flights attained reflect the state of the sport at that time; in a contest admittedly restricted to *ab initio* flying, the winner put in a prize-winning flight of 27 seconds.

Not all gliding clubs had simple names and Stirling was home to The Central Scotland Air Yachting Club which operated from King o' Muirs Farm, Tullibody near Alloa. Meanwhile something of a milestone was reached when, on September 6th, 1931, 30-year-old Newcastle-born Charles Herbert Lowe-Wylde crossed the Firth of Forth in a two-seat BAC VII having been aero-towed by a Moth to 4,000 feet creating the star turn for Edinburgh Gliding Club's air pageant staged at Silverknowes, Davidson's Mains. His flight was no simple effort for the tow-cable jammed and he could not release it. In the end the Moth pilot released it from his end, leaving the entire cable dangling under Lowe-Wylde's glider. He had been aiming for Donibristle but with a hard-to-control mount he flew a mile east of the Forth Bridge and found a field at Rosyth about half a mile from his target.

Aviators have always enjoyed a strangely macabre sense of humour and some contemporary local wit penned this mournful couplet, more limerick than Burns:

A Norful Tragedy
There was a young lady called Norah,
Who snored as she soared on a soarer.
On a lone Highland moor,
There's a trifle of gore,
And the world is a Norah the poorer.

Most of these clubs bought their gliders either from Germany or, increasingly, from the newly-formed British companies such as BAC Ltd at Maidstone in Kent, or RFD in Guildford and E D Abbott at Farnham, both in Surrey. Because damage was a recurrent event, all groups rapidly gained experience at glider repair to the point where many felt competent to build their own machines from scratch, copying existing models or buying sets of plans for the popular if very basic Dickson glider.

By the end of 1931 many clubs had been established across Scotland with some thriving like Falkirk, Edinburgh and Border, others such as Kilmarnock having too few members to buy a glider but hard at work building their own. Some of the problems these avant-garde clubs faced are exemplified in the tale of the Border club for, when the lambing season began, they were prevented from flying and had to move to another field on the Edinburgh road three miles north of Hawick!

Meanwhile the Central Scotland Air Yachting Club had been touring around Stirling in ever-widening circles. Ideal sites were not always matched with friendly farmers so forcing a decision to use a field east of Alloa at an altitude of 900 feet above sea level. Even this was restricted by escarpments on several sides. You clearly had to be very keen to glide in those days as was clear from the Glasgow Club which was forced to change sites frequently often having nowhere at all to fly despite having two gliders and another under construction. Finally, in 1932, it secured a permanent site near Paisley and the dreaded 'notices to quit' became things of the past.

This somewhat hit-and-miss operation by a number of clubs across the nation was not ideal. Few clubs were large enough to be able to afford modern gliders and proper support equipment and the gliders they had were mainly obsolete trainers. During the early part of 1934, a number of the Scottish clubs got together to consider the future. The result was the formation of the Scottish National Gliding Club at the end of June. With all existing clubs pooling resources Scotland would at last have a meaningful gliding movement. On July 7th, everybody gathered at Miss Buick's Tea Rooms in Glasgow's West George Street for the inaugural meeting of what was already being called the Scottish Gliding Union.

While the revived movement had all the enthusiasm it could require, it really needed money and it was some little while before it got going. Having considered many sites accessible to Edinburgh, Glasgow, Stirling and Falkirk it finally settled on a site at Kilsyth in conjunction with the old Falkirk club's site.

As the simple and rather basic sport of downhill gliding gradually developed and systematically moved into the realm of hill and thermal soaring flight, this maturing encouraged more to explore the theory and practice of their sport which had, at that time, largely been developed in Germany. In June of 1935 many watched as a German-built Schleicher Rhönadler high performance single seat competition sailplane was winched into the air by a converted Model T Ford at Renfrew.

The following year Joan Meakin (*aka* Mrs Ronald Price) had taken Britain by storm with her aerobatics in her Wolf sailplane. Then, in 1937, Andrew J Thorburn of Kirkcaldy became the first sailplane private owner in Scotland with his Falcon I which he flew at Bishop Hill achieving flights in excess of one hour's duration and ascending to 5,000 feet.

By this time, gliders were rapidly improving thanks to better aerodynamics and, it has to be said, lessons learned from the enthusiastic Germans who frequently visited to take part in competition flying in Britain.

The art of soaring and the skills of manipulating weather and terrain to the best effect soon established Scotland as an ideal gliding venue.

On July 15th, 1938, the Scottish National Gliding Club was incorporated as a limited liability company but little more than a year later all came to a stop with the outbreak of war. Much of the equipment, including gliders, was commandeered by the Air Ministry for use by the newly-formed Air Defence Cadet Corps. By 1946 it was clear that the movement was depleted not just by equipment but, sadly, by many of its founding people. It fell to Andrew Thorburn and two men from Edinburgh, Robert Parker and William Lawson, to revitalise the Scottish Gliding Union Ltd on Balado Airfield near Kinross.

Here the SGU blossomed and expanded for eleven years until the increasing use of Kinross by the Royal Air Force necessitated another move, this time to Portmoak Farm close to Scotlandwell, by Loch Leven. Ultimately the SGU was able to buy the whole farm and so secure its own airfield.

In more recent times a number of new groups have sprung up such as the Lanarkshire & Lothian Soaring Club formed in 1975 to serve the Glasgow-Edinburgh area. Today there are around a dozen gliding venues across Scotland.

SUMMARY

Scotland has been to the forefront of every aspect of aviation since earliest times. While it has never actively participated in the 'space race', it has played a major part in the development of navigational aids, radar and telecommunications. The large number of pictures that follow expand much of the story so far merely outlined. The majority have not been published before.

Her Majesty the Queen has always taken a keen interest in the Royal Air Force and, in 1951 when still Princess Elizabeth, she went to Leuchars and presented 43 Squadron with a Standard. Half a dozen years later she flew to Leuchars in a RAF Comet T.2 XK669 (formerly G-AMXB *Taurus* which was then modified for 216 Squadron at Lyneham in 1955). This was her first flight in the pure-jet transport and here we see her and the Duke of Edinburgh arriving, having flown from RAF Marham, near Sandringham, in 50 minutes at a speed of 360 mph. On this occasion she again presented a Standard to 43 Squadron.

AIRLINES IN SCOTLAND

a Chronological List of Major Commercial Operators

NORTH BRITISH AVIATION CO LTD. A touring joy-riding and air-show operator which flourished between 1930 and 1935.

BRITISH FLYING BOATS LTD/BRITISH AMPHIBIOUS AIRLINES LTD. Reg. June 23rd 1932 by Kirston & Mace Operated occasional service with Saro A.17 Cloud on Stranraer – Belfast and Greenock – Belfast. *Fl.*1932-1933.

SCOTTISH MOTOR TRACTION CO LTD. Founded Edinburgh, mid-1932. Air charter service based Renfrew. Closed autumn 1934.

HIGHLAND AIRWAYS. Registered Edinburgh by Edmund E Fresson on April 3rd 1933. In May of 1935 control passed to **UNITED AIRWAYS** which, on August 12th, 1937, merged with **SCOTTISH AIRWAYS LTD.**

MIDLAND & SCOTTISH AIR FERRIES LTD. Founded March 10th, 1933, by John and Christina Sword; based Renfrew; folded 30th Sept 1934. John Sword was also a director of **SCOTTISH MOTOR TRACTION CO LTD** but companies were separate entities.

ABERDEEN AIRWAYS LTD. Registered Edinburgh by Eric Leslie Gandar Dower January 2nd 1934. On February 13th 1937 renamed **ALLIED AIRWAYS (GANDAR DOWER) LTD** through to start of War. Later absorbed by **BRITISH EUOPEAN AIRWAYS.**

ALLIED AIRWAYS. *See under* **ABERDEEN AIRWAYS LTD.**

LONDON, SCOTTISH & PROVINCIAL AIRWAYS LTD. Registered February 7th 1934; surveyed route London to Renfrew that March but did not operate, moving south instead.

RAILWAY AIR SERVICES LTD. Registered on March 21st 1934 by rail companies. Operational to May 1940 when all routes absorbed by **ASSOCIATED AIRWAYS JOINT COMMITTEE** but continued in operation by RAS. By September 1946, RAS was working closely with **BRITISH EUROPEAN AIRWAYS CORPORATION** into which it officially merged on February 1st, 1947.

NORTHERN AIRWAYS LTD. Founded by George Nicholson on July 1st 1934, at Cramlington Airfield, Northumberland. On November 21st, 1934, became: **NORTHERN & SCOTTISH AIRWAYS LTD** and shifted operations to Renfrew. *See also under* **SCOTTISH AIRWAYS LTD.**

NORTHERN & SCOTTISH AIRWAYS LTD. Founded on November 21st 1934 by George Nicholson. Evolved from **NORTHERN AIRWAYS LTD.** Taken over by Whitehall Securities Ltd in 1936 and, with **HIGHLAND AIRWAYS** and **UNITED AIRWAYS**, was absorbed into **BRITISH EUROPEAN AIRWAYS** in 1946.

UNITED AIRWAYS. Founded in May 1935 by Whitehall Securities which was merged with **SPARTAN AIRLINES, HIGHLAND AIRWAYS, NORTHERN & SCOTTISH AIRWAYS** and **SPARTAN AIRCRAFT LTD,** and later became **BRITISH EUROPEAN AIRWAYS.**

WEST OF SCOTLAND AIR SERVICES LTD. Business founded at Renfrew mid-1935 by Glyn Roberts. In April 1937 name changed to West of Scotland Airways Ltd. Operated one DH.83 G-ACCT which was finally sold to Australia. No further details.

ALLIED BRITISH AIRWAYS LTD. Company created on September 30th, 1935 for the purpose of merging the publicly quoted company Hillman's Airways with the private companies of Spartan Air Lines and **UNITED AIRWAYS LTD**, both controlled by the Hon. Clive Pearson's Whitehall Securities Corporation Ltd. On October 29th, 1935, the name was changed to **BRITISH AIRWAYS LTD**, and on December 11th, 1935, it converted to a public company.

BRITISH AIRWAYS LTD. The original company was **ALLIED BRITISH AIRWAYS LTD** created in 1935 by the merger of Spartan Air Lines, **UNITED AIRWAYS** and Hillman's Airways. It became a public company on December 11th, 1935. In April 1936 the airline merged with British Continental Airways, operating under the name **BRITISH AIRWAYS.** The London terminal was Gatwick but on February 7th, 1937, all services were transferred to Croydon Airport. Prior to the outbreak of war in 1939, the Government had already implemented the Air Navigation (Restriction in Time of War) Order 1939 under which it was ordered the military takeover of most civilian airfields in the UK, cessation of all private flying without individual flight permits, and other emergency measures. It was administered by a statutory department of the Air Ministry titled National Air Communications. By September 1st, 1939, the aircraft and administrations of **BRITISH AIRWAYS LTD** and Imperial Airways were physically transferred to Bristol (Whitchurch) Airport, to be operated jointly by NAC. On April 1st, 1940, **BRITISH AIRWAYS LTD** and Imperial Airways Ltd were officially combined into a new company, British Overseas Airways Corporation (BOAC) which had been set up on November 24th, 1939. The name would lie moribund until the creation of the new company on March 31st, 1974.

NORTH EASTERN AIRWAYS LTD. This company first appeared in 1935 but was restructured in November 1936, Based in London it operated services along the east coast of England to Edinburgh, Perth and Aberdeen including a service to Glasgow during the duration of the 1938 Empire Exhibition at Wembley, Middlesex.

ALLIED AIRWAYS (GANDAR DOWER) LTD. Founded February 13th, 1937. Remained outside the jurisdiction of the **ASSOCIATED AIRWAYS JOINT COMMITTEE** during the war years and having made its own arrangements with the British Government, operated its own services from Aberdeen to the Orkney and Shetland Islands.

WESTERN ISLES AIRWAYS LTD. Founded on July 19th, 1937; became holding company for **SCOTTISH AIRWAYS LTD** on August 12th, 1937 as a 50% owned subsidiary. Operations suspended with outbreak of war. Became part of **BRITISH EUROPEAN AIRWAYS** on February 1st, 1947.

SCOTTISH AIRWAYS LTD. Incorp as private company on August 12th 1937; formed out of **NORTHERN & SCOTTISH AIRWAYS LTD** (temp named **NORTHERN AIRWAYS**) and **HIGHLAND AIRWAYS** to co-ordinate the internal interests of British Airways Ltd. Holding co was **WESTERN ISLES AIRWAYS LTD**, formed July 19th, 1937, changed into holding co on August 12th, 1937.

ASSOCIATED AIRWAYS JOINT COMMITTEE. War-time operators of airline services decreed to be of 'national importance' which included most of the Scottish Island routes. Founded May 5th 1940, the AAJC took over operations from a number of airline companies, those concerning Scotland being **RAILWAY AIR SERVICES, SCOTTISH AIRWAYS LTD**, and **WEST COAST AIR SERVICES LTD.**

BRITISH EUROPEAN AIRWAYS CORPORATION. Formed on January 1st, 1946 as the British European Airways Division of British Overseas Airways Corporation. Became a Crown Corporation on August 1st, 1946. On February 1st, 1947, BEAC took over **ASSOCIATED AIRWAYS JOINT COMMITTEE (AAJC)** of which **RAILWAY AIR SERVICES, SCOTTISH AIRWAYS (Highland and Western Divisions), NORTH EASTERN AIRWAYS** and **WESTERN ISLES AIRWAYS** were part. Initially based Croydon and Northolt with DH.89a Dragon Rapides and Douglas DC-3 aircraft. Moved operations to Heathrow from April 1950. Merged with British Overseas Airways Corporation in 1974 to form British Airways Ltd.

BRITISH UNITED AIRWAYS LTD. Formed mid-1960 by the re-naming of the old company of Airwork Ltd. Created by Nigel Norman and Alan Muntz in 1928, Airwork had developed Heston Airport, West London, pre-war. During the 1939-45 war, was responsible for aircraft maintenance, pilot training & airline work. After the war Airwork acquired independent airline Transair and, in conjunction with Hunting-Clan, expanded its airline operations forming **BRITISH UNITED AIRWAYS** which included Airwork Helicopters, Air Charter, Bristow Helicopters, Channel Air Bridge, Transair and Morton Air Services.

CALEDONIAN AIRWAYS LTD. Scottish charter airline formed April 1961 with head office at Crawley, West Sussex. The idea of Adam Thompson, former **BRITISH EUROPEAN AIRWAYS** pilot and friends, Specialised in 'affinity group' transatlantic charters. Highly successful operator, always profitable. Merged with in 1970 and restyled **BRITISH CALEDONIAN AIRWAYS.**

LOGANAIR LTD. Founded at Glasgow Airport (Renfrew) on February 1st, 1962, by Duncan McIntosh initially as the air taxi service of the Logan Construction Company Ltd. In 1964 Loganair began an inter-island scheduled network in Orkney, and a similar network in Shetland in 1970. It took on more remote islands and communities. After the closure of Renfrew, the business moved to Abbotsinch in 1966 at the same time becoming a Limited Liability Company, and a year later established an Air ambulance service covering Coll, Colonsay, Oronsay, Mull and Oban. These operations ceased on March 31st, 2006, when the contract shifted to Gama Aviation. Taken over by what became the Royal Bank of Scotland, between 1968 and 1983, the airline expanded its route network, helped by the decision of British Airways to 'rationalise' some of its 'thin' routes to Loganair, and in 1980 Loganair took over the Belfast to Edinburgh route from BA. During the 1990s the company became associated with the British Midland Group but with its subsequent reorganisation in 1994, some of Loganair's cross-border services were transferred to Manx Airlines (Europe) and the formation of British Regional Airline (BRA) Ltd. Meanwhile Loganair became British Airways' second franchise operator. On July 8th, 2011, Loganair agreed to acquire Cambridge based Suckling Airways (Cambridge) Ltd trading as ScotAirways (founded 1986). This company is now part of Loganair.

STRATHALLAN AIR SERVICES LTD. Charter company founded in 1963 at Strathallan Castle, Auchterarder, Perthshire, by Sir William Roberts. Briefly operated a scheduled service to the Shetland and Orkney Islands. Managing director was Capt Peter D Tunstall. Business faded c.1970.

PEREGRINE AIR SERVICES. A business incorporated in Glasgow on November 8th, 1965, at Kintyre House, 209 West George Street. On January 6th 1988 advertised for pilots with the tag of 'the longest established air charter company in Scotland with an unbroken record of operations since 1969'. The company was based at Dyce, Aberdeen. It appears to have been regenerated that year out of the remains of **AIR ECOSSE** with offices at Inverness, but ceased operations on dissolution on October 5th, 1996.

BRITISH CALEDONIAN AIRWAYS. Founded in 1970 by the amalgamation of **CALEDONIAN AIRWAYS LTD** and **BRITISH UNITED AIRWAYS.** In December 1987 was taken over by newly-privatised **BRITISH AIRWAYS.**

AIR ECOSSE. Commuter airline founded in June 1977 at Aberdeen with London offices at 6, Bloomsbury Square, to service needs of the North Sea oil industry. Began scheduled commuter services on July 1st, 1979, flying between Aberdeen and Liverpool and Carlisle, Edinburgh and Glasgow. A subsidiary of the Fairflight Group of companies of Biggin Hill (formerly Blackbushe and originally by AVM Donald C T Bennett). Declining business forced stop to operations in the Spring of 1987 and, despite plans for reorganisation, it entered administration in 1988. Was bought out by **PEREGRINE AIR SERVICES** of Aberdeen and the new company became **ABERDEEN AIRWAYS LTD** (not to be confused with the pre-war Gandar Dower firm of the same name).

MALINAIR Ltd. Commuter airline founded in June 1985, started operations out of Glasgow early 1986. Prime route was Glasgow-Donegal. Developed network with former **AIR ECOSSE** staff. Despite grand expansion plans, operations ceased in the autumn of 1987.

HIGHLAND EXPRESS. Founded Prestwick for daily service to Newark. First schedule July 4th, 1987; folded a few months later.

SCOTTISH EUROPEAN AIRWAYS. Founded Paisley on April 27th, 1988 offering services between Brussels, Frankfurt, Newcastle, Edinburgh and Glasgow. Folded mid-1990.

ABERDEEN AIRWAYS LTD. Formed 1996 out of Peregrine Air Services but soon in financial trouble. After move to East Midlands and finally disappeared. No connection with the pre-war airline of a similar name associated with Gandar Dower.

One of the promotional posters for the Lanark event. Contestants pre-registered for the event included Gustav Blondeau, E Colmore, Graham Gilmour, James Radley, Marcel Hanriot, Armstrong Drexel, Lancelot D L Gibbs, Cecil Grace, Maurice Edmond, Rene Vidart, Robert Svendsen, Bartolomeo Cattaneo, GŽo Chavez, Samuel Franklin Cody, Edmond Audemars, George Bertram Cockburn, Bertram Dickson, William McArdle, Alec Ogilvie, George A Barnes, G P Kuller, Maurice TŽtard, Florentin Champel, Howard Joseph Harding and Edmond Morel. Most of these were the household names of the age and the youngest entrant was Marcel Hanriot, fifteen years old and flying one of his father's aircraft. In the end, Maurice TŽtard did not show up; B C Hucks did.

Alliott Verdon Roe's Triplane was a casualty of the railway company en-route to Lanark when sparks and embers from the engine ignited the tarpaulin covering it on an open, flat-bed wagon. Such was the enterprise shown by the pioneering aviators of the age that despite what would appear to be a major set-back, Roe had his machine rebuilt and flying in time for the Ayrshire event. Note the name 'AVROPLANE' on the fuselage. This aircraft is a good example of the philosophy of the time that did not restrict the centre of gravity to a percentage of the wing chord for at this time it was thought quite acceptable for the rear wings to take their share of the lift. The aerodynamic effect of this was that recovery from a stall would be extremely difficult, while manoeuvrability would be compromised by the associated increase in fuselage drag. In those days, everybody was still learning!

Samuel Franklin Cody (1867-1913) was a curious, charismatic character. Circus performer, showman and man-lifting kite-developer, he built and flew the first successful powered aircraft in Britain at Farnborough in October 1908. How did he become 'Colonel' Cody? The King, on addressing him on one occasion, mistakenly referred to him as 'Colonel' Cody. From that time on, Cody said 'if the King thinks I am good enough to be a colonel, then colonel I shall be' – or words to that effect. He certainly never was one, although he was treated with respect by all in the world of aviation. Here we see him at the Lanark meet parked outside his named hangar in the row of similar named sheds with their open canvas doors. His giant aeroplane was nicknamed 'the cathedral' allegedly because of its size. This was not strictly so. Most aircraft had wings that swept upwards a little at the tips and this was called *dihedral*. If the wings were straight or dipped down at their tips, the opposite of 'dihedral' was 'kathedral'. And Cody's aircraft had that *kathedral* wing form. Today we would use the more modern form – *anhedral*. Cody's performance at Lanark was not distinguished because his aircraft was underpowered. It made only a few short flights. Two years later, his 120 hp Austro-Daimler powered Military Competition Biplane was outright winner of the Military Trials. In 1913, while flying his floatplane, he crashed and was killed, earning a funeral in Aldershot with full military honours as would befit a much-loved colonel... *Picture from the collection of Richard Stenlake.*

Cody was, like all pioneers, a self-trained flyer and aircraft-builder who was the senior figure at the time of the Lanark meet. American-born in 1857, his family name was actually Cowdery and his early life was spent as a cowboy and entertainer. He first came to the attention of the Army at Aldershot with his kites, especially when he devised the principle of 'chaining' a number of kites to a common rope to lift great weights. He took to designing and building aircraft and gained the Royal Aero Club's ninth pilot's licence. Always known as 'Colonel Cody', the handle stayed with him to the day in 1913 when his aircraft collapsed in mid-air killing both him and his passenger, the now-forgotten cricketer William Evans (born 1883). By that time, Cody was a naturalised British citizen. His showing at Lanark was not brilliant since his 65 hp engined aircraft proved underpowered. He took off eventually after a very long run, cleared the rough ground that had claimed Dickson's Boxkite, alighted on a distant slope – and taxied safely back to his shed to tumultuous applause! Strong winds for the rest of the week saved Cody from further attempts but on the final Saturday evening, the wind had dropped sufficiently for Cody to have another attempt and this time he managed to fly twice round the course. Here he is seen sitting in his machine showing the large tanks, one for water and the other petrol. Remember that engines were water-cooled, hence very heavy for their power output.

One of the notable figures of pre-First War aviation was the handsome B C Hucks. Bentfield Charles Hucks (1884-1918) piloted the first aeroplane to be seen in the skies over Aberdeen when, on August 29th, 1912, he was pictured on this post card image 'flying over the Bathing Station'. The picture is heavily retouched and is most probably a fake, but even so was published to record the actual event. Hucks' unusual first name comes from the name of the village where he was born, Bentfield near Stansted in Essex. He is widely remembered for none of these details but for the fact he gave his name to the motorised aeroplane-starter based on a Ford truck with a powered and adjustable overhead shaft that engaged with the propeller hub. *Picture from the collection of Richard Stenlake.*

At this time, portraits tended to be eschewed in favour of the more 'dramatic' cockpit shots like this. B C Hucks had been the first Briton to 'loop-the-loop' (as the manoeuvre was popularly called) in November 1913 and became a notable early pilot in the RFC ending the war with the rank of captain. A fine and creative life was cruelly cut short just after the war: that November he was cut down in the Spanish 'flu epidemic.

The Lanark meeting was 'covered' by the issue of many postcard images such as this one. Straight ahead is the shed of the 'Official Photographer' advertising 'post cards 4/-' presumably for a pack of some quantity. The side of the shed bears a poster reading 'Lovely North Wales Resorts; Travel via Caledonian and N W Rys'. To the right, in front, is a kiosk bearing the sign 'Aviation postcards on sale here'. The picture is meant to illustrate the Chilean-born American Cecil Grace (1880-1910) flying over the heads of the spectators. The lack of detail, the presence of a halo around the aircraft and a rather incongruous perspective reminds us that the camera can lie and this 'photograph' is, in fact, a superimposition of another image into the clear sky area of another! Even so, Grace was to win a massive £1,950 of prize money at Lanark – almost a quarter of the £8,000 prize money put up by the Glasgow Evening News. After Lanark, Grace became a British citizen and, tempted by Baron de Forest's £4,000 prize for the longest flight from England into mainland Europe, set off from Eastchurch on December 22nd. Bad weather dogged him to Calais where he stopped for lunch before heading back home to make a fresh start another day. He was never to be seen again. *Picture from the collection of Richard Stenlake.*

A friend of the Wright Brothers, Alexander 'Alec' Ogilvie was a Londoner born in 1882 who became only the seventh person to qualify as a pilot. Alec Ogilvie demonstrated the latest Short-built Wright Biplane with a wheeled undercarriage at Lanark. One great problem with early wheels on aircraft was that they were usually taken from bicycles or motorbikes which meant that while they might take the weight they had insufficient resistance to a side load. If the aircraft landed with a small degree of sideways drift, the wheel that touched first would simply buckle and fold under. Combine a heavy landing with drift and the wheels became a hindrance rather than a help to a safe landing. Whereas wooden skids might withstand such use without damage, it was the collapse of wheels that caused more damage to aircraft in these early days. Not until special aircraft wheels were developed which had wide hubs and well-splayed heavy spokes was this risk allayed. Ogilvie, unlike too many of his contemporaries, survived into old age, dying at Ringwood, Hampshire, in 1962. He was 80 years old.

Although not a Scot, Graham Gilmour was the most popular aviator of his day largely because of his daredevil approach to his sport. Born in Dartford, Kent, in 1985, Gilmour quickly took to flying and bought a two-seat BlŽriot Monoplane with which he proceeded to make a name for himself. As a motorist he was always at loggerheads with the authorities and, in answering one speeding case, flew to the court in his aircraft, endearing himself to the judge so much that, after fining him 10/-, he invited him home for tea. But then Gilmour flew low over the Henley Regatta, rolling his wheels in the River Thames, so earning a Royal Aero Club one-month ban. Then he flew dangerously low over the 1911 University Boat Race and got reprimanded, flew low over the Houses of Parliament, circled the steeple of Salisbury Cathedral and was cautioned – and so on. Gilmour was the bad boy that everybody secretly admired and so it was when he came to Lanark. More popular than the flamboyant, if talented, Yankee flyer Armstrong Drexel, more 'of the people' than the ebullient Colonel Cody – and less of a Scottish demi-laird than Dickson, when Gilmour came third in the 'getting-off' contest at Lanark, the cheering was deafening. In this picture, the judge in the foreground appears to perform a cake-walk in delight! In those days, take-off was called either 'pulling up' (which, confusingly, meant stopping in motoring terminology) or 'getting off' which, in popular street jargon, was nothing at all to do with flying – at least, not in aeroplanes. Poor Gilmour, like Dickson, was not in for a long life. On February 17th, 1912, he was flying a new type of aircraft from Brooklands on a cross-country flight. The weather was perfect as he crossed Richmond Park when horrified people watching from the ground saw both wings fold upwards and the aircraft plummet into the park. Gilmour died not through his reckless high spirits, but by structural failure of his aircraft. At his death, his total wealth amounted to just £22.10/-. He had lived his brief life to the full!

An early use of airport ground equipment in Scotland is pictured here at the Lanark meeting. Edinburgh's Captain Bertram Dickson had given a faultless display in his Bristol Boxkite on the opening Saturday, achieving a distance of 12 miles 776 yards in the distance flight challenge with a fine landing despite the fitful gusty wind. On Sunday, of course, there was no official flying although some testing was undertaken. On Monday Dickson decided to attempt a maximum weight flight and so took to the air with a passenger. Together the two weighed 25 stone 4 lbs but Dickson wanted to carry more than 180 kilogrammes as an experiment, so he added between three and four stones of sheet lead wrapped around the skids. The aircraft took off successfully and climbed well until, beyond the brow of a hill beyond the judge's box, gusts and downdraughts forced them into a landing in very rough ground with a ditch running across it. The machine touched down but one skid ran into the ditch and tipped the aircraft, breaking both wings on one side and the front elevator. Here Lanark's Bucephalus retreats with his cartload of spoil from Dickson's Hydaspes – proof that despite this flying nonsense the horse remains more than just a reliable stand-by. As for the splintered Boxkite, it was repaired and flying again shortly afterwards.

John William Dunne's contribution to aviation is sometimes questioned by those who do not recognise how far ahead in time was his thinking. Described as 'destitute of a sense of humour' and 'deficient in the sense of proportion that usually goes [with humour]' (see Percy Walker: *Early Aviation*, Vol.2, p.233), Dunne fervently believed that a pilot should not have to fight for control of his aircraft and that auto-stability was a vital necessity. At that time – and for a long while later – most would have agreed with that statement. Only in recent years do we deliberately eschew stability for the fighter jet's inability to do absolutely anything without the firm (and dubious) hand of a hidden computer system. Here is a rare picture of Dunne's powered tailless biplane of 1908 – the D.4. It is being tested at the subsidiary testing grounds in Blair Atholl village, a site which is today a caravan park.

Normally annotated pictures are the annoying province of low-brow daily papers that cater for readers who don't understand what they are looking at. However, in the case of *The Illustrated London News*, they rightly considered that posterity would like to be reminded of the parts of the unfamiliar Dunne. Soon after this picture was taken, the Gnome rotary was replaced by a four-cylinder upright Green. This picture is from the issue dated August 23rd, 1913.

Test-flown extensively by two highly-experienced pilots, Colonel John Edward Capper and Captain John Valentine Carden, the Dunne Biplane was without doubt inherently stable. Dunne, who was not himself a flyer, claimed that the pilot merely had to direct the machine and he did not have to *fly* the machine. Possibly an over-simplification but by all accounts the Dunne was far easier and safer to fly than a conventional aircraft of the time. This was dramatically demonstrated in this aircraft when on one occasion the solo pilot vacated his cockpit in mid-flight and proceeded to climb in and out of the rigging of the wings. All the while the aircraft continued to fly straight and level and the pilot finally resumed his seat for the landing. And yet what had started out so promisingly in Perthshire was allowed to die a sad death at the hands of the War Office myrmidons. The inventor of this extraordinary aircraft licensed its manufacturer to the French Nieuport firm as well as to Burgess in the US where it was developed into a successful floatplane. Scotland's loss, England's shame – and an early bonus for the Yanks!

Disillusioned by the British rejection of his design, John Dunne licensed his aircraft design first to France and then America while he himself withdrew from aviation. In the US, that country's first-ever licensed aircraft manufacturer eagerly took up Dunne's brilliant concept. W Starling Burgess and Greeley S Curtis founded their company at Marblehead, Massachusetts, in 1910 and built Wright Biplanes under contract, some fitted with pontoon floats. In 1912 the name of the business changed to The Burgess Company and a year later they were building Dunne Biplanes. The US Navy acquired some in 1914 under the designation AH-7 while one was sold to Canada where it was lauded as 'Canada's First Military Plane'. That self-same aircraft survives in a museum in Ontario – a distant reminder of those Perthshire trials, a lost British opportunity – and a great inventor who was snubbed. This aged photograph was taken on March 18th, 1914, and shows a US Navy Dunne on pontoon floats. Note the anchor motif on the wing tip curtain. Also visible in this old snapshot is the progressive washout of the wings towards their tips.

The British Army wasn't all that struck on conventional aeroplanes. It believed solidly in balloons and kites for the good reason that these devices could carry telephones so you might converse with your observer as he peered through binoculars 500 feet above you. Now you couldn't do that with a flying-machine, now could you! Meanwhile the kelpies in Whitehall had little idea what shape an aeroplane should be so almost immediately after rejecting the Celtic Dunne's inherently safe tailless aeroplane, the Balloon Factory at Farnborough (which was still trying to work out which end of an aircraft the tail ought to be positioned at) launched into the building of the SE.1. Unbelievably this was a rebuild of a crashed Army BlŽriot monoplane. The new aeroplane was not only a biplane but a canard having a large tail surface at the front, twin rudders carried on outriggers and a pusher engine in the shape of a 60 hp water-cooled ENV. Balloon Factory superintendent Mervyn O'Gorman had high hopes for this hybrid when it was rolled out in June 1911 but it proved to need consistent tweaking. Unlike the Blair Atholl experience, the SE.1 (which stood for 'Santos Experimental Number One') was anything but stable. O'Gorman's assistant as superintendent was 36 year-old Lieutenant Theodore John Ridge who had just learned to fly and amassed several hours of experience. He had already made one more or less successful flight in the machine. On August 18th he begged to be allowed to fly the SE.1 again after it had been pulled back to its starting point as pictured here. He took off, side-slipped into the ground, destroyed the SE.1 and succumbed to his injuries. SE.1 RIP!

Most of the early aeroplanes did not enjoy long lives. This was mainly because they were frail in construction and were scarcely fit for purpose. Add to that mixture the fact that pilots were generally long on enthusiasm and short on training and you have a situation which is foreign to longevity. Maurice Farman S.7 Longhorn No.207 was powered by the usual 70 hp Renault engine and was flown from Hendon to Farnborough on August 14th, 1912, by the noted French pilot Pierre Verrier and, after acceptance, it went to No.2 Squadron. In the hands of Captain George William P Dawes it was one of the machines which participated in the epic flight to Montrose. When it went to the Northern Ireland Army Manoeuvres it was damaged beyond repair at Ballyhornan on September 24th.

Another of the machines which made Montrose that September was this BE.2a, No.267, taken on charge on March 18th 1913 but wrecked a month later. In its rebuilt state Lieutenant Leonard Dawes got it safely to Montrose. The following summer it flew south, this time to Netheravon and, after more damage and rebuilding, it went to Hounslow and joined No.1 Reserve Aeroplane Squadron.

This Maurice Farman S.7 Longhorn, serial number 266, was taken on charge on December 21st, 1912 and allocated to No.2 Squadron, then at Farnborough (right next to Aldershot where our previous picture was taken) and about to transfer to Montrose. On the epic flight there it was piloted byLieutenant P W L Herbert. It reached Montrose on February 26th and is seen here at the original Montrose aerodrome at Upper Dysart Farm. Notice the temporary canvas hangars. No.266 crashed on May 5th, 1913 and went back to the Royal Aircraft Factory for repair before being transferred to the Central Flying School as No.472. *Picture from the collection of Richard Stenlake.*

When No.2 Squadron RFC arrived at Montrose there were absolutely no facilities or hangars and the aircraft had to be parked out in the open – not something these rather flimsy early aircraft appreciated. If it rained, the fabric covering was not totally waterproof and could become waterlogged adding weight to the aircraft. Conversely, exposure to hot sunlight would split the fabric where it passed around a sharp edge. While a simple post and rope fence keeps most of the local young and old at bay, it remains a splendid scene of barely visible organisation. It is February 1913. *Picture from the collection of Richard Stenlake.*

Built at the Royal Aircraft Factory, Farnborough, the three BE.2a aeroplanes seen here with a Maurice Farman S.7 pusher at the far end, have been picketed down for the night against the shelter of some trees for the night at Montrose (Dysart), No 272, nearest the camera, was taken on charge by No.3 Squadron on March 20th 1913 and was flown by Major Henry Robert Moore Brooke-Popham (later to become Air Chief Marshal) on April 9th. It was then reallocated to No.2 Squadron and, between May 19th and 21st, Captain John Harold Whitworth Becke of the Sherwood Foresters flew it to Montrose. It was then flown to Ireland via Castle Kennedy for the Irish manoeuvres that September before returning to Montrose on October 1st. The following June 4th the aircraft crashed en route to Netheravon but although repaired seems to have done little subsequent flying. *Picture from the collection of Richard Stenlake.*

Some 32 miles north north east of Montrose, Aberdeen's golf links presented one of Montrose's pilots with a landing opportunity. At 10.15 on the morning of Saturday April 18th, 1914, golfers and observers all over the town were in thrall at the sight of a Maurice Farman Longhorn as it swooped low over Napier's yard and rolled its wheels to an easy landing on the hallowed turf. Within minutes the crowd of young and old alike thronged across the greensward. Players were prevented from driving from the tee to the Cowhillock green due to the mass of rubber-neckers. After half an hour, the unnamed pilot restarted his engine and made a graceful take-off and headed back south. This machine had already experienced some adventures. Positioned conveniently, if not equidistantly, between Northern Ireland, the Isle of Man, Prestwick, Blackpool and Carlisle, Castle Kennedy Airfield today claims to be the only facility for general aviation in the south west of Scotland although it is not actually licensed and after use as a go-karting track, has settled down to occasional PPO/PPR operation at pilot's discretion. It was not always so for, in 1913, as Cult's Farm, it was first used by aircraft of No.2 Sqdn RFC at Montrose as a stopping-point for preparation to cross the Irish Sea. To help in the event of a ditching, the flight comprising one Maurice Farman MF-7 flown by Captain George William Patrick Dawes (1880-1960) Dawes (pictured here), and five BE.2 aircraft, were fitted with flotation bags to assist them in the event of trouble over the Irish Sea. The crossing was undertaken on September 2nd and it was the first time a unit of the RFC had flown overseas. It was not without its problems, though, one BE.2 pilot being forced to return to adjust his engine. Even so, the other four pilots landed safely at Rathbone near Limerick. At the conclusion of the exercise only three of the original six aircraft were able to complete the journey from Castle Kennedy to Montrose, the remainder having suffered from mechanical or navigational problems. Positioned three miles east of Stranraer, Castle Kennedy later became home to a busy RAF FTS section, but closed after the Second World War. *Picture from the collection of Richard Stenlake.*

Caldale Air Station was a Royal Naval Air Service base to the west of Kirkwall, Orkney. It was built between 1915 and 1916, being commissioned in July, 1916. Prime feature were the two large iron-covered timber-framed airship sheds visible right of centre in this picture which shows the station accommodation huts. The hangars housed Submarine Scout Pusher (SSP) airships which were used for anti-mine and submarine spotting sweeps around Orkney. The geographic location was hardly suited to the operation of such large and vulnerable vessels. Thus it was that during November 1917, two of its airships – SSP-2 and SSP-4 – were both caught by high winds and destroyed. Even worse, the latter vessel's crew were lost at sea. There were at least two more incidents involving damage by wind soon afterwards so the Admiralty shut down the station and moved its surviving airships to more sheltered sites on the Scottish mainland. Early in 1918 the station's hangars were used for the repair of kite balloons and became the home for No. 20 Kite Balloon Base. With the end of the war, the operation was run down and finally closed in 1920. *Picture from the collection of Richard Stenlake.*

Launching a Maurice Farman Seaplane (120 hp Renault) at Cromarty in July 1913. Serialled 117, this was assembled on July 12th and test-flown two days later by Lieutenants A M Longmore and Douglas Austin Oliver. On October 2nd that year Longmore flew it with Winston Churchill as passenger but five days later it was completely wrecked leaving 'nothing but the tailplane worth repairing'. This rare photograph shows how the aircraft was manhandled down a wooden slipway into the water. New South Wales-born Arthur Murray Longmore (1995-1970), later awarded the DSO, would become Air Marshal Sir Arthur and, by 1936, held the position of Air Officer Commanding Coastal Command. During the Second World War he attained the rank of air chief marshal. *Picture from the collection of Richard Stenlake.*

First War wooden-framed hangars at Montrose form a panoramic backdrop to this Avro 504K aircraft being flown solo as it approaches to hand. *Picture from the collection of Richard Stenlake.*

When War broke out in 1914 it was painfully evident that Britain's established aircraft factories could not cope with the likely demand for new machines. Quickly sub-contractors were sought ranging from those that could manufacture components to those who could handle the building of complete aircraft. With its wide range of manufacturing skills, Glasgow was well-placed for the second category and shipbuilders Alexander Stephen & Sons Ltd of Linthouse, already collaborating with engineers G & J Weir of Cathcart, swiftly shifted to production of the Royal Aircraft Factory's BE.2c design. Bearing the service serial number 4500 (pre-dating the introduction of a letter prefix), this was the first of 50 aircraft to roll off the production line in August 1915. The engine had yet to be fitted. *Picture from the collection of Richard Stenlake.*

Pictured in the mid-'thirties, the officers' quarters at Montrose were well-established. The white stones lining the edges of the roadways remind generations of servicemen of the old adage 'if it moves, move it; if it moves by itself, salute it; and if it don't move – then paint it!' Although considered somewhat isolated geographically, Montrose was considered a prestige posting in those days. *Picture from the collection of Richard Stenlake.*

Training accidents have always been a factor of learning to fly and they were all-too were common during the First World War. Here is an Avro 504K which has distinguished itself with a spectacularly bad landing at Lesmahagow in South Lanarkshire. This type of mishap was normally survivable for both occupants and aircraft and the aeroplane would be repaired and back in the air within days. *Picture from the collection of Richard Stenlake.*

Forgotten flyers from a distant age. Airmen of 'C' Flight, No. 1 RFC School of Aerial Fighting & Gunnery at Turnberry, Ayrshire, stand before a Bristol F2.B Fighter. Turnberry had been a golf course set up by the Marquess of Ailsea in the early 1900s but the land was commandeered soon after the First World War broke out in 1914 because of its flat prospect. One of the instructors here for a while was Major James McCudden, later to earn the VC. At the end of the war, the land returned to being a golf course but, with the start of World War Two, the land was once more turned into an RAF airfield, this time with three concrete runways. As home to 618 Squadron it saw use by Bristol Beaufighters on patrol duties with Coastal Command and was later home to Liberator bombers. Now once more it is a golf course although reparations after the last war needed to be far more extensive than those required after the first. *Picture from the collection of Richard Stenlake.*

A singularly rare image is this one showing the Short S.14 Sarafand six-engined flying boat at anchor near Craigie Stane, Lerwick. Developed from the Short Singapore II, the Sarafand was at the time the largest aircraft ever built in the British Isles. Launched from Short's Medway factory at Rochester in Kent, it made its first flight on June 30th, 1932 at the hands of test pilot John Lankester Parker with designer Oswald Short as co-pilot. The six 825 hp Rolls-Royce Buzzard engines were arranged in pairs – three as tractors, three as pushers – in between-wing nacelles. Only one example was built and S1589 carried out evaluation trials at the Marine Aircraft Experimental Establishment, Felixstowe. Until this photograph emerged, its visit to the Shetlands was unrecorded. *Picture from the collection of Richard Stenlake.*

The star of the 1924 Lympne Light Aeroplane Competitions in Kent was undoubtedly the Dalmuir-built Beardmore Wee Bee which the magazine *The Aeroplane* described as 'one of the most astonishingly efficient aeroplanes yet produced'. Flown by Maurice Piercey, the No.4 competitor exceeded everybody's expectations and was the outright winner of the Air Ministry's first prize of £2,000. Furthermore it emerged as one of only two aircraft in the whole contest reliable enough to complete the high speed trials. Pilot Piercey clocked a staggering 70.1 mph. Beardmore's aircraft division, which played a dominant role in the Great War, had closed down in 1920 after the Beardmore-Rohrbach Inflexible was built, but with the opportunity of Lympne looming, the company set up a fresh aircraft section and hired Yorkshire-born William Stancliffe Shackleton as chief designer. Shackleton had already proved his worth in the previous year's competition when he worked as the designer for ANEC. His solution for Beardmore was an aeroplane to a similar formula – a true ultra-light aeroplane with a tiny 30 hp Bristol Cherub two-cylinder motor. The contest was to find the ideal training and club aeroplane and in this respect it was a failure for the contest rules failed to acknowledge that for such a role both structural robustness and adequate engine power were the vital prerequisites.

October 8, 1924 — The Aeroplane — 359

BEARDMORE MONOPLANE WINS

Sport & General Photo.

The Air Ministry 1st Prize of £2,000

"No more efficient Aeroplane than the Beardmore Aeroplane (which won the chief prize) has ever left the earth," stated Lt.-Col. W. A. Bristow, the aeronautical consulting engineer, who kept the records of the competitions.

Margin of speed is a very good standard of efficiency in an aeroplane, and this machine has a very wide margin. It can fly at about 90 miles an hour and also under 40 miles an hour. It can rise from the ground quickly and pull up slowly.

THE TIMES,

LIGHT AEROPLANE TRIALS.

THE LYMPNE RESULTS

SUCCESS OF BEARDMORE MONOPLANE.

(FROM OUR AERONAUTICAL CORRESPONDENT.)

LYMPNE, OCT. 4.

The Beardmore Wee Bee monoplane, flown by Mr. M. Piercey, and fitted with an ungeared Bristol Cherub engine, won the first prize of £2,000 offered by the Air Ministry at the Light Two-seater Aeroplane Trials which concluded here to-day. The Bristol Brownie monoplane, flown by Mr. C. F. Uwins, also fitted with an ungeared Cherub engine, secured the second prize of £1,000.

BEARDMORE MONOPLANE WITH CHERUB ENGINE

WILLIAM **BEARDMORE** AND COMPANY LIMITED

Dalmuir, near Glasgow, Scotland.

London Office - - - - 36, Victoria Street, S.W.1.

That series of contests held in Southern England in an attempt to find the ideal light aeroplane are remembered today for their ill-judged comprehension of what a light aeroplane actually was (by the organisers) and the wonderful aircraft talented designers produced to comply with those badly-drafted rules! One of the amazing designs that resulted came from the Beardmore works. Even more remarkably, it was a champion winner! Pictured at the Royal Aero Club Meeting at Lympne in August 1925 by the ABC engine designer Granville Eastwood Bradshaw (1887-1969) himself is this view of the Beardmore Wee Bee G-EBJJ and its Bristol Cherub engine together with its associated personnel. The Wee Bee was the outright winner of the £2,000 prize money in the 1924 Lympne Light Aeroplane Trials – a great feat for so small and lightly-constructed an aircraft. The tall figure, second from left, is Beardmore's chief test pilot, Flight-Lieutenant Archibald Norman 'Bill' Kingwill who, along with Maurice Walter Piercey, did much of the flying. Third from left is Flight Lieutenant David Forgham Anderson who had, four years earlier, survived the crash of the new Central Centaur 4a which had been assembled with crossed elevator cables. Standing close to the nose is designer William Stancliffe Shackleton. The car at the left is Sir William Beardmore's own Beardmore Galloway 10/20 of 1924.

William Beardmore & Company Ltd rightly shouted news of its win from the roof-tops! The proud Scottish firm took a whole page advertisement in *The Aeroplane* for October 8th, 1924.

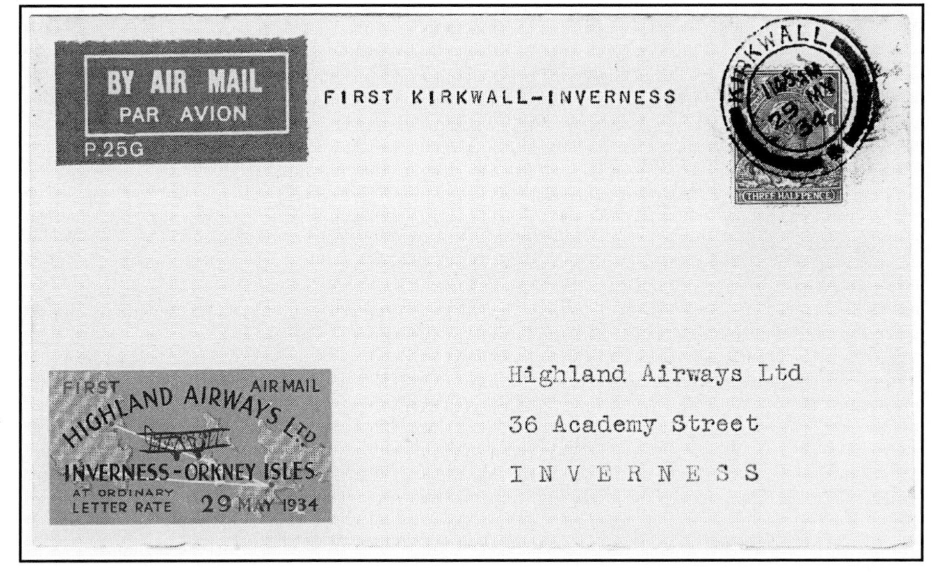

Many stamp-collectors collect 'first-day covers' – envelopes that have the significance of having been used to mark the inauguration of either a new postage stamp or an event. Here is a rare piece – an envelope that was carried in DH.84 Dragon G-ACCE by Captain Fresson on the first flight from Kirkwall to Inverness – airmail where only surface carriage had previously been available. It is one of over 2,000 letters he carried when he received the first internal service postal pennant from the then Director of Postal Services, Sir Frederick Williamson. Postmarked May 29th, 1934, it also bears the Highland Airways' carriage label and is addressed to the firm's own Inverness address, 36 Academy Street, today a sports shop.

John Neilan joined Aberdeen Airways in February 1936 as third pilot after James Gordon Hay. Eric Allen Starling was chief pilot. Neilan was born John Charles Stuart Wortley Neilan in 1911 and previously worked as a pilot for De Havilland Aircraft Company. Besides flying, he took many photographs, preserving images of the places he visited and items of interest he overflew. The waters around Orkney have claimed many vessels that have been drawn onto their perilous rocks and many of these he pictured from his de Havilland DH.84 Dragon. The wreck of the *Neptunia* in February 1936 and, a month later, the trawler *Siberite* at Hoy were all captured this way. He made a low pass over the ferry *St Ola* crossing the Pentland Firth in command of Captain Swanston and circled low around the Dunnet Head lighthouse for another photo. Here is his mount, G-ADFI, a Mk.II with framed windows. Named *The Silver Ghost*, it had been modified to have a powerful landing lamp in the nose which did nothing to improve the angular lines of the Dragon. Neilan was also an accomplished glider pilot and holder of numerous British gliding records.

Thurso's Claredon Aerodrome in all its glory as pictured looking east from about 800 feet from the cockpit window of John Neilan's G-ADFI. The three white strips immediately in front of the hangar are sheets of plywood laid down on the normally muddy soil to enable an aircraft to be pushed into the hangar. At the top of the picture is Stiffley Farm. Today this is a picturesque if deserted, ivy-clad ruin. Apart from a new house on the north side of the old farm and a small cluster of new homes north of the A836 at the lower left of the picture, the site is little changed from 80 years ago.

Designed originally for Edward Hillman's Hillman Airways, the de Havilland DH.84 Dragon was specified by its bus-company owning first customer as to be 'a low-cost and cheap twin-engined version of the Fox Moth'. Initially it was called the Dragon Moth but soon the appendix was elided. The prototype Dragon was G-ACAN which first flew at Stag Lane on November 12th, 1932. Hillman had already extended his low-cost service from Essex to Glasgow. The rotund, sanguine complexion'd Hillman was a character in the aviation world. Ill-educated and bluntly outspoken, he was accustomed to running motor coaches and buses and he treated his low-cost airline and its pilots as little more than another bus route with a driver up front. But when at the end of 1934 he suddenly died at the height of his O'Leary-like career, he was greatly mourned and even *The Aeroplane*'s Charles G Grey penned a fulsome tribute to his achievements. His airline became one of those that merged to form the original British Airways. But already he had outgrown his Dragons and re-equipped with the four-engined DH.86, nicknamed the Express, G-ACAN went to Eric Leslie Gandar Dower's Aberdeen Airways Ltd. Named Starling after his chief pilot, the aircraft commenced a regular service from Aberdeen to Orkney via Wick and Thurso in May, 1935. The base at Dyce was small and aircraft servicing had to be spread between available premises. Here the Dragon is wedged into the small hangar at Thurso for maintenance. The outer wings (which could be folded back) have been removed and the fuselage and centre-section just fits into the available space. The two-gallon petrol cans lined up in the foreground form the available fuel supply. Note how the hangar doors open on rails and park along the front half of each inner side.

Aberdeen Airways' chief pilot was the legendary Eric Allen Starling (1911-1997) seen here with the company's DH.84 Dragon Mk.II, G-ADFI, and pictured at Thurso on February 22nd, 1936, by John Neilan. Starling was born in London and had an interesting and unusual flying career having started as an apprentice pilot with Croydon's Redwing Aircraft Company. Gaining his commercial licence in 1933, he set off to fly from Croydon in Surrey to Lympne on the Kentish south coast but got hopelessly lost as darkness fell and fog arose. Finally, low on fuel, he spotted a brightly-lit and wide street – so he landed on it. To his and everybody else's astonishment he found he was in Calais! He later became a pilot in a flying circus before meeting Gandar Dower who offered him the job with his newly-formed airline based at the newly-built 'Granite City's' aerodrome. He went on to experience a distinguished flying career during the war after which he joined Scottish Airways which later became BEA. He died aged 85 in 1997.

Parked on the grass at Thurso Aerodrome, John Neilan's Aberdeen Airways' Dragon G-ADFI awaits its next sortie. Note the ancient gabled bothy behind the newly-built wooden hangar. The field, also known as Claredon Aerodrome or Stiffley Farm, was first used on June 11th, 1935, and was in use until the Spring of 1940. You will still find the open land recognisable beside the Thurso-Castletown road (A836) but there is no trace whatsoever of the hangar. The bothy, now a roofless shambles, survives. As for the aircraft, this met its end in a crash at the aerodrome on July 3rd, 1937: it struck a wall and burst into flames but not before everybody escaped unharmed.

West Lothian's Kirknewton Aerodrome as photographed by John C Neilan with his 116-size folding Kodak camera from Lanton Hill in 1934. Some 13 miles south west of Edinburgh, it was surveyed as a diversion for Edinburgh but was seldom used since it was 'meteorologically challenged' more than other and more useful sites. It was, however, developed during the war as an early satellite to Royal Air Force Turnhouse and was used occasionally by a RAF Reserve Flying Training School.

Scotland was not alone in offering pilots challenging operating conditions and Aberdeen Airways' pilot John C Neilan took his camera with him wherever he went. His collection of photographs, in the present author's collection, includes ship-wrecks off the Orkneys, sea-tossed ferries heavy-weathering grim passengers in high seas – and challenging air strips on his routes. This shot, from the cockpit of his Dragon Rapide, shows the landing strip at Groomsport north east of Bangor in County Down. There is no trace of this rectangular field today in what is now a heavily built-up area of Northern Ireland.

As Aberdeen Airways' business grew, it began to re-equip with more modern airliners and late in 1935 along came the DH.89 Dragon Rapide with its streamlined form and bigger engines. Registered on May 7th, 1935, G-ADDE was named *The Aberdonian* and delivered by John C Neilan to Dyce on October 31st, 1935. The occasion merited a staff line-up photograph. From the right is pilot Neilan, next is Gandar Dower and then chief pilot Eric Starling and Agnes Thompson, Aberdeen's first female MD and Gandar Dower's friend. Next is Gander Dower's partner, Caroline Brunning. The two gentlemen at the back are radio officer Alec Milnes and engineer Cecil Goodall. The aircraft later served with North Eastern Airways before being impressed as X9386 on June 4th, 1940. It saw communications duty throughout the war years and on March 24th, 1947, was sold back to Eric Gandar Dower. It was not, however, reinstated to the Civil Register and one presumes that it was deemed not worth restoring for a civil certification.

Wick Aerodrome is about as far north as Scotland extends. The field was used by Fresson for his Highland Airways Ltd (later Scottish Airways Ltd) operations from 1933 to 1939. He operated services from Inverness (Longman) via Wick to Kirkwall (Wideford). Its position on the north east tip of the mainland provided an excellent striking-off point for services to the Orkneys and the distant Shetlands. Again it became a vital RAF base during the war with hard runways and the other trappings of an active air base. None of that, however, is visible in this picture of Dragon Rapide G-AGSK operated by British European Airways in 1947. The concrete blocks in the foreground were used as tie-downs to protect these comparatively light aircraft from being blown away in the strong winds that prevailed. *Picture from the collection of Richard Stenlake.*

Aberdeen's first aerodrome was at Seaton where Fresson operated his early Highland Airways services from. Soon afterwards he moved to a better field at Kintore where he established a 'permanent' base. When Eric Gandar Dower wanted to share the field, Fresson refused and Gandar Dower immediately set up his own field at Dyce. In the end, it was Dyce, a field established in 1934 as part of Gandar Dower's strategy to link the northern isles with London, that stood the test of time. It became a significant RAF base during the war before being nationalised in 1947 and subsequently taken over by British Airports Authority in 1976. This evocative photograph shows a line-up of visiting and resident aircraft about 1935-36. Besides Moths and Avians, G-ACKZ, far right, is a DH.83 Fox Moth registered on November 7th, 1933. It was sold to India in January 1938 becoming VT-AJW. *Picture from the collection of Richard Stenlake.*

Scottish Motor Traction Co Ltd was based in Edinburgh but established a flying base at Moorpark Aerodrome, later to become Glasgow-Renfrew. Founded as a bus company, in 1932 it formed an aviation department and began operations in April 1933. The company had commendable ideas on commercial flying and decided that all aircraft had to be bought new from their manufacturers, all must carry full instrumentation including two-way radio and landing lights – neither being mandatory at that time. The chairman and managing director was Wellington John Thompson (1869-1937), Lord Provost and Lord Lieutenant of the City of Edinburgh. The business operated an eight-strong fleet of Fox Moths, a Tiger Moth, a Dragon and four Avro Cadets but during 1934 business dwindled and eventually all the aircraft were sold off. *Picture from the collection of Richard Stenlake.*

Midland & Scottish Air Ferries Ltd was registered in Edinburgh on March 10th 1933 by John C Sword and Christina C Sword of Craigweil, Ayr. Actually the company operated its first routes several weeks earlier with a 7-day long scheduled air service from Hooton Park, Cheshire, to Birmingham's Castle Bromwich to convey visitors to and from the British Industries' Fair staged in Birmingham. A connecting service operated as an air taxi between Hooton Park and Liverpool with a DH.83 Fox Moth. Registered on May 12th, 1933, this DH.84 Dragon I, G-ACDL, was delivered to John Sword's company and employed on a service from Renfrew via Campbeltown to Islay (Bridgend) three times a week. Islay's original airport was on the beach at Loch Indaal. The 8-passenger Dragon (initially known as the Dragon Moth) was one of the fourteen aircraft Midland & Scottish operated during its eighteen months of existence. John Sword had tried hard but in the end simply ran out of money. His business ceased on September 30th, 1934. The venerable Dragon changed hands several times before being sold to the Spanish Republicans in August 1936. *Picture from the collection of Richard T Riding.*

John and Christina Sword's Midland & Scottish Air Ferries operated no fewer than four DH.83 Fox Moths. One, G-ACCU, is seen here at an unidentified location (possibly Renfrew) in 1934. It seems to be some sort of company promotional flight and the man seated in the cabin is holding a large camera, the lens of which is supported by the fellow standing alongside. *Picture by E J Riding from the collection of Richard T Riding.*

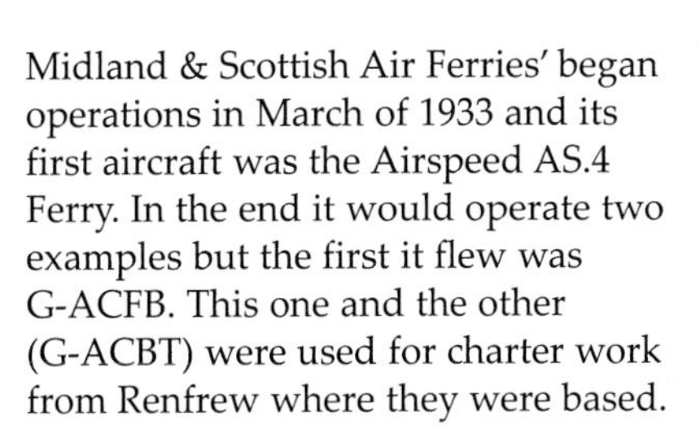
Midland & Scottish Air Ferries' began operations in March of 1933 and its first aircraft was the Airspeed AS.4 Ferry. In the end it would operate two examples but the first it flew was G-ACFB. This one and the other (G-ACBT) were used for charter work from Renfrew where they were based.

Midland & Scottish Air Ferries Limited was a private company with £20,000 nominal capital. Its centres of operation were Hooton Park aerodrome in Cheshire and Glasgow's Renfrew Aerodrome. It began with two Airspeed Ferry three-engined biplanes (G-ACBT and G-ACFB) and quickly grew so that soon it was operating a mixed fleet of some sixteen aircraft of seven different types. One was this Avro 631 Cadet, G-ACIH, pictured at Renfrew. This aircraft survived the war in sheltered but not secure storage, its fuel tanks filled with sand to deter theft and in March of 1961 was sold to Matthew Pearse Cahill, the son of Hugh Cahill, founder of Iona National Airways, Ireland's first commercial airline (1931-1995). It became EI-ALU and is reputed to be in existence and undergoing a long-term restoration.

An aspect of operating from unprepared fields that is oft overlooked today is the amount of dirt the aircraft would acquire. Apart from muck thrown up by the wheels and lower propellers (usually a healthy mixture of filth and flies cemented to the aircraft by cow-dung), there was also the problem, (with the Airspeed Ferry) that the top engine dripped oil which would spread right down the fuselage top and, occasionally, the sides. In those days before detergents, the only thing to clean this off was petrol. Here one of Midland & Scottish Air Ferries' Airspeed Ferry triple-engined transports is having a good scrub. Note the open passenger door to the cabin under the cranked lower wing root.

Another of the Midland & Scottish Air Ferries' fleet was this de Havilland DH.84 Dragon Mk.1, G-ACCZ, pictured at Bridgend, Islay in 1933. The 'airfield' was in truth the beach at Loch Indaal which offered an amply-large area of well-drained and level sand at low water. *Picture from the collection of Richard Stenlake.*

Northern & Scottish Airways Ltd was founded on November 21st, 1934, to operate services in western Scotland from Glasgow's Renfrew Airport. The business was founded by the enterprising Newcastle bus operator, George Nicholson. An airstrip was opened on the Isle of Islay at Glenegedale in the early 1930s. This picture was taken in July 1934 on the occasion of a visit to Islay by members and aircraft of the Renfrew-based Scottish Flying Club. Curiously the airport sign misspells the name of the locale. By 1940 the grass strip had been developed into Islay Airport with paved runways. Glenegedale gained a measure of notoriety on June 29th, 1994, when the Prince of Wales, piloting a BAe 146 (ZE 700) of No 32 (The Royal) Squadron RAF, overshot on landing and made national news in the ensuing pile-up. He was unhurt: the aircraft was not so lucky damage was described as 'substantial'. *Picture from the collection of Richard Stenlake.*

A panoramic view of Glenegedale looking westwards over a line-up of visiting aircraft in the summer of 1934. *Picture from the collection of Richard Stenlake.*

Northern & Scottish Airways was based at Glasgow (Renfrew). For its summer schedule in 1936 it produced this green and black pocket timetable cut out in the shape of a DH.84 Dragon's profile. The fare structure and the baggage allowance makes interesting comparison with some of the services on offer today.

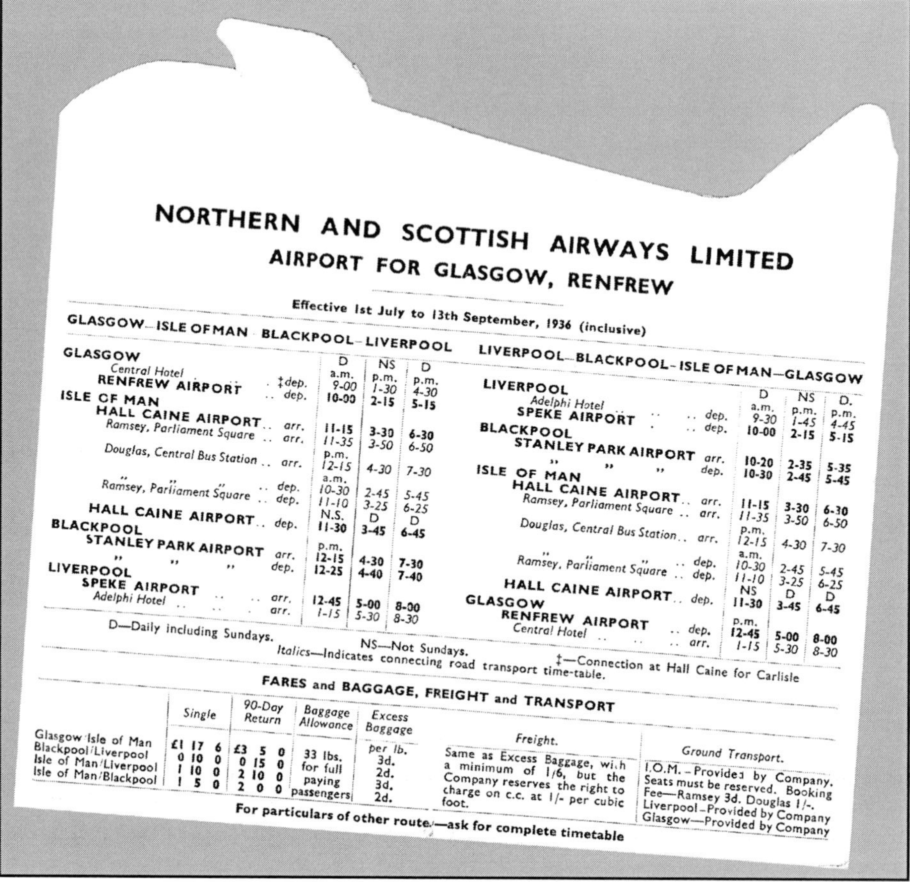

NORTHERN AND SCOTTISH AIRWAYS LIMITED

AIRPORT FOR GLASGOW, RENFREW

Effective 1st July to 13th September, 1936 (inclusive)

GLASGOW—ISLE OF MAN—BLACKPOOL—LIVERPOOL

		D	NS	D
GLASGOW		a.m.	p.m.	p.m.
Central Hotel	‡dep.	*9-00*	*1-30*	*4-30*
RENFREW AIRPORT	dep.	**10-00**	**2-15**	**5-15**
ISLE OF MAN				
HALL CAINE AIRPORT	arr.	**11-15**	**3-30**	**6-30**
Ramsey, Parliament Square	arr.	*11-35*	*3-50*	*6-50*
Douglas, Central Bus Station	arr.	p.m. *12-15*	*4-30*	*7-30*
" " "	dep.	a.m. *10-30*	*2-45*	*5-45*
Ramsey, Parliament Square	dep.	*11-10*	*3-25*	*6-25*
		N.S.	D	D
HALL CAINE AIRPORT	dep.	**11-30**	**3-45**	**6-45**
BLACKPOOL				
STANLEY PARK AIRPORT	arr.	p.m. **12-15**	**4-30**	**7-30**
" " "	dep.	**12-25**	**4-40**	**7-40**
LIVERPOOL				
SPEKE AIRPORT	arr.	**12-45**	**5-00**	**8-00**
Adelphi Hotel	arr.	*1-15*	*5-30*	*8-30*

LIVERPOOL—BLACKPOOL—ISLE OF MAN—GLASGOW

		D	NS	D.
LIVERPOOL		a.m.	p.m.	p.m.
Adelphi Hotel	dep.	*9-30*	*1-45*	*4-45*
SPEKE AIRPORT	dep.	**10-00**	**2-15**	**5-15**
BLACKPOOL				
STANLEY PARK AIRPORT	arr.	**10-20**	**2-35**	**5-35**
" " "	dep.	**10-30**	**2-45**	**5-45**
ISLE OF MAN				
HALL CAINE AIRPORT	arr.	**11-15**	**3-30**	**6-30**
Ramsey, Parliament Square	arr.	*11-35*	*3-50*	*6-50*
Douglas, Central Bus Station	arr.	p.m. *12-15*	*4-30*	*7-30*
" " "	dep.	a.m. *10-30*	*2-45*	*5-45*
Ramsey, Parliament Square	dep.	*11-10*	*3-25*	*6-25*
		NS	D	D
HALL CAINE AIRPORT	dep.	**11-30**	**3-45**	**6-45**
GLASGOW				
RENFREW AIRPORT	dep.	p.m. **12-45**	**5-00**	**8-00**
Central Hotel	arr.	*1-15*	*5-30*	*8-30*

D—Daily including Sundays. NS—Not Sundays. *Italics*—Indicates connecting road transport time-table. ‡—Connection at Hall Caine for Carlisle

FARES and BAGGAGE, FREIGHT and TRANSPORT

	Single	*90-Day Return*	*Baggage Allowance*	*Excess Baggage* per lb.
Glasgow/Isle of Man	£1 17 6	£3 5 0	33 lbs. for full paying passengers	3d.
Blackpool/Liverpool	0 10 0	0 15 0		2d.
Isle of Man/Liverpool	1 10 0	2 10 0		3d.
Isle of Man/Blackpool	1 5 0	2 0 0		2d.

Freight. Same as Excess Baggage, with a minimum of 1/6, but the Company reserves the right to charge on c.c. at 1/- per cubic foot.

Ground Transport. I.O.M.—Provided by Company. Seats must be reserved. Booking Fee—Ramsey 3d. Douglas 1/-. Liverpool—Provided by Company Glasgow—Provided by Company

For particulars of other routes—ask for complete timetable

A busy scene at London's Croydon Airport in August of 1935. Centre is G-ACSM, one of the Spartan Cruiser Mk.II airliners operated by Northern & Scottish Airways of Renfrew having completed its Glasgow-London schedule. To the left is de Havilland DH.84 Dragon G-ACDL of Midland & Scottish Air Ferries, also just in from Glasgow. To the right is a second Spartan Cruiser, G-ACSM belonging to British Airways.

Northern & Scottish Airways operated a number of West Coast routes including Glasgow-Belfast-Isle of Man-Blackpool-Liverpool, Carlisle-Isle of Man, Glasgow-Campbeltown-Islay and Glasgow-Skye-North Uist-South Uist-Barra-Benbecula-Glasgow. For Easter, 1937, it went to the expense of producing an attractive ten-page three-colour little holiday timetable of services. Regarding the Skye service which landed at Glenbrittle Airport, a note adds that 'tea and sandwiches, etc., can be obtained at Glenbrittle House at usual prices'. The Glenbrittle aerodrome was opened on December 5th, 1935 and closed at the outbreak of war and was not used again.

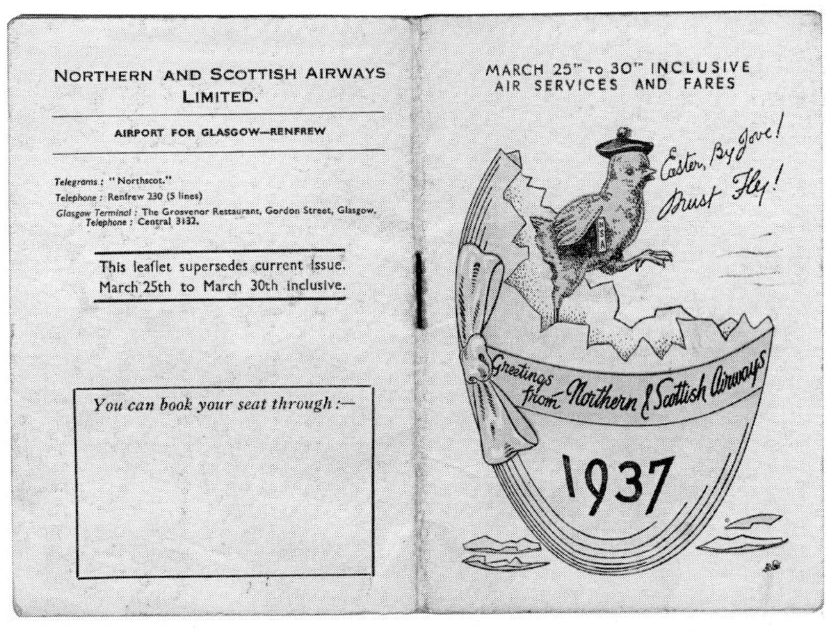

NORTHERN AND SCOTTISH AIRWAYS LIMITED.

AIRPORT FOR GLASGOW—RENFREW

Telegrams: "Northscot."
Telephone: Renfrew 230 (5 lines)
Glasgow Terminal: The Grosvenor Restaurant, Gordon Street, Glasgow. Telephone: Central 3132.

This leaflet supersedes current issue.
March 25th to March 30th inclusive.

You can book your seat through:—

MARCH 25TH TO 30TH INCLUSIVE
AIR SERVICES AND FARES

Easter, By Jove! Must Fly!

Greetings from Northern & Scottish Airways

1937

Spartan Cruiser Mk.III G-ADEL served with Northern & Scottish Airways Ltd at Renfrew, and later Scottish Airways Ltd. One of only three built of this model, like its predecessors it suffered from rear fuselage/tailplane oscillations: note the heavy bracing struts to the fin. Impressed on May 3rd, 1940, it became X9432 during the war but was scrapped two months later due to the discovery of advanced airframe deterioration.

Edmund E Fresson's first Kirkwall landing field was at Wideford but what would become the later Kirkwall Airport was not opened until 1940 as RAF Grimsetter, an outpost for the defence of the Scapa Flow naval base. It was transferred to the Royal Naval Air Service in 1943 at which time it was re-named RNAS Kirkwall, later HMS Robin. It was taken over by the Ministry of Civil Aviation in 1948 for the expansion of the air service to the islands. During 1986 it was reassigned to Highlands & Islands Airports and became a major civil airport used by the Flybe franchise service run by Loganair. It is remembered for being the location of an embarrassing accident to Vickers Viscount G-BFYZ of Alidair. On October 25th, 1979, the aircraft was approaching to land after a flight from Abbotsinch in bad weather with gusting cross-wind. The pilot decided to correct the misalignment of his approach at a low height. The Number 4 propeller struck the runway on touchdown and the aircraft ran off the right side of the tarmac. The nosewheel collapsed when encountering the edge of an intersecting runway. The airliner veered off into the softer yonder. While none of the 51 people on board was hurt, the aircraft was a constructive write-off. At the subsequent inquiry it was said that 'the accident was caused by the commander failing to take overshoot action at an early stage in the approach to land when it became apparent that the approach was unstabilised and the windscreen wiper was unreliable.' A bit like the proverb 'For the want of a nailÉ' *Picture from the collection of Richard Stenlake.*

One should always be suspicious of picture postcards purporting to depict early aircraft. Card publishers were very good at darkroom techniques such as superimposition. This postcard shows a de Havilland Dragon flying towards Loch Indaal from Islay and sharing space with the Round Church at Bowmore. A nice picture – but perhaps not strictly right! Bowmore's unusual church, built in 1767, stands on high ground above Jamieson Street and looks north-west across the water. *Picture from the collection of Richard Stenlake.*

G-AETM was a de Havilland DH.86B four-engined airliner registered on June 29th 1939 to Allied Airways Ltd, of Woolsington, Newcastle. Given the name *Silver Star* it was used by Gandar Dower in the years immediately before the outbreak of the 1939-45 War. In December of 1939 it went to Finland as OH-SLA and then, following conversion to Air Ambulance status as OH-IPA, to the Finnish Air Force. Operated by Suomen Ilmavoimat, on May 2nd,1940, it was damaged beyond economic repair in a non-fatal take-off accident at Helsinki's Malmo Airport when it collided with Brewster B-239E fighter BW-394.

Like many small airlines throughout Britain, many started with the de Havilland Dragon and then up-graded to the DH.89 Dragon Rapide. Allied Airways (Gandar Dower) Ltd was established in 1937 and on July 12th it began a five times a week service between Newcastle and Norway using a de Havilland DH.86B Express, the four-engined biplane. Meanwhile, the twin-engined DH.89 Dragon Rapide was the interior-routes workhorse. Allied Airways eventually had seven examples, this one, G-ACZF, being built in November 1934 and thus one of the earliest made. It survived the war years and is seen here with passengers at Aberdeen in the early part of 1946 when it carried the name *Carina*. *Picture via Emily Stratton.*

Pictured at Glasgow's Renfrew Airport in May of 1946, G-AGOJ was a Dragon Rapide of Scottish Airways Ltd. Formerly NR774, it was civilianised and gained its C of A on April 27th, 1945. It lasted until May 1st 1961 when it crashed at Lympne. Prior to that it had served well on the inter island services but did not survive to become one of the British European Airways' fleet. *Picture by E J Riding from the collection of Richard T Riding.*

Renfrew was the place to see Rapides in the immediate years after the war, Scottish Airways' Dragon Rapide G-AGIF (X7336) is seen here parked outside one of the big hangars in May 1946. These were the difficult years when British European Airways was newly formed and about to assume all the internal air routes from the old-established operators like Scottish Airways (Highland and Western divisions), Railway Air Services, North Eastern Airways and Western Isles Airways. BEA's dominance began in February 1947 and before that Easter it had absorbed Allied Airways (Gandar Dower) Ltd. As for G-AGIF, this was scrapped at Newtownards on January 24th, 1950. Its remains languished behind the hangar until April 1954 when it was burned. *Picture by E J Riding from the collection of Richard T Riding.*

A cold day in February 1947 as two Scottish Airways Dragon Rapides are parked on the apron awaiting duties. G-AGJG was originally X7344 and was brought to the civil register at the end of 1943. G-AGLE, behind, was NR 685 and joined the civil register in December 1944, serving well until crashing at Morden in Surrey on March 17th 1949. *Picture by E J Riding from the collection of Richard T Riding.*

Pictured at Renfrew in 1938, by which time it was owned and operated by Airwork Ltd, is Jim Mollison's former record-breaking DH.80a Puss Moth, G-ABKG. He flew from Lympne on March 24th, 1932, and reached the Cape in four days 17 hours and 19 minutes. For the attempt, the aircraft had been modified as a single-seater, the rest of the cabin space being given over to a long-range fuel tank. Mollison's next Puss Moth was even more of a radical change from the standard: it had extra windows in the rear of the cabin so the pilot could fly from the back seat while the entire front was a 160-gallon main fuel tank giving the Stag Lane product a range of 3,600 miles. Meanwhile, G-ABXG, seen taxiing in the wet with a guide on the starboard wing tip, was later impressed as W6416 on January 2nd, 1940, then within a week being converted to an instructional airframe as 2068M. An ignominious end for a great aircraft. If only wings could talkÉ

Operating a schedule in wintertime has always been a challenge and looking back it seems astonishing that flights were seldom delayed and rarely cancelled due to operational conditions. Seen here in the winter of 1936 are two of Railway Air Services' DH.89 Dragon Rapides. Nearest the camera is G-AEAL *Star of Yorkshire* and next to it is G-AEAM, *Star of Ulster*. From the passengers' point of view, the Rapide did not have a heated cabin and warmth depended on clothing. Note that the provision of the nose landing light was standard. During the ten years of its production, 728 Rapides were built and no direct replacement was available until the arrival, in 1967, of the Britten-Norman Islander. Incidentally, the designation DH.89a was applied to all Dragon Rapides after G-AEOV because these had trailing edge flaps fitted to the lower wings.

The three-engined Spartan Cruiser, built at Cowes on the Isle of Wight and derived from the so-called Saro-Percival Mailplane, was used by Railway Air Services. Here G-ACSM, a Mk.II model built in 1934) comes in to land at Glasgow's Renfrew Aerodrome in 1936. This aircraft was impressed into the RAF as X9433.

Spartan Cruisers were built in East Cowes by the Spartan Aircraft Company, an offshoot of Saunders-Roe Ltd. The all-metal Mk.III was the last of the development and was originally made for Spartan Air Lines based at Cowes as a subsidiary company of the actual manufacturers. Railways Air Services took over the routes and aircraft Spartan had operated after its absorption by British Airways Ltd in 1936. Four other Cruiser Mk.III aircraft were then taken over by Northern & Scottish Airways Ltd at Renfrew and were operated on services to the Highlands and Islands until the start of war in 1939. On August 12th, 1937, N&SA was temporarily renamed Northern Airways which then became incorporated in Scottish Airways. G-ADEL, pictured here at Renfrew in 1937, was duly transferred to Scottish Airways Ltd in January 1937 before being impressed as X9432 in April of 1940. However, its Service life was brief: on July 26th it was found to have extensive rot in both fuselage and mainspar and was officially struck off charge. *Picture from the collection of Richard Stenlake.*

Pictured at Renfrew in 1936 is the updated Spartan Cruiser Mk.III, G-ACYK, seen here on climb-out. Note the heavily-trousered undercarriage. Again operated by RAS, this machine went on to serve with Scottish Airways but was lost in a crash at Largs on January 14th, 1938. Its surviving remains were recovered by helicopter in July 1973 and are today on display in the Scottish Museum of Flight at East Fortune.

A still-camouflaged Dragon Rapide with the name of Railway Air Services in a white band on the nose. The registration, G-AGLP, is in wartime configuration with an underscore of red, white and blue lines. This was one of three Rapides used by RAS for its Anglo-Scottish services. This machine operated the first southbound Prestwick-Croydon service on April 9th 1945, departing Prestwick at 9.40 in the morning and arriving at Croydon at 13.50 with stops en route at Renfrew and Liverpool Speke Airport for refuelling. The aircraft were based at Renfrew and this photograph shows the first London flight on its arrival at Croydon Airport. *Picture from the Richard Riding Collection.*

One of the more outlandish creations of the 1930s was the Short-Mayo Composite which comprised a four-engined seaplane named *Mercury* (G-ADHJ) mounted on top of a four-engined flying-boat named *Maia* (G-ADHK). The brainchild of Major Robert Hobart Mayo, technical general manager of Imperial Airways, later to be a designer at Shorts, it was intended as a super-fast mailplane combination. Shorts had already introduced its Empire flying boats which could operate long range routes across the British Empire. The real target, though, was the Transatlantic route and here the problem was balancing fuel with payload. Yes, the crossing could be made with full tanks, but the payload was minimal. Increase the payload and the range would suffer. Mayo reckoned that he had the answer based on the fact that, once airborne, an aircraft could maintain flight with a greater load than it was possible to take off with. His idea was to mount a small, long-range seaplane on top of a larger carrier aircraft, using the combined power of both to bring the smaller aircraft to operational height, at which time the two aircraft would separate, the carrier aircraft returning to base while the other flew on to its destination. It was a cumbersome idea and obsolescent while still on the drawing-board, but Short Brothers went ahead and the aircraft flew well both as individual machines and as a combination while the intricacies of in-flight separation were practised with aplomb. The real test was what the maximum duration of the seaplane might be. To find out, the combination flew to Dundee, alighting in the shallow Tay where, as this snapshot shows, it attracted public attention. With *Mercury*'s floats filled (for take-off) with fuel, *Maia-Mercury* took off on October 6th, 1937, and climbed to 4,700 feet. With *Mercury* at a gross weight of 27,500 lbs and at a wing-loading of 45 lbs/sq,ft – far higher than most other contemporary aircraft – cast free and headed south across Fife in the hope of reaching Cape Town in one hop. Australian-born pilot Donald Clifford Tyndall Bennett (1910-86) encountered severe head-winds over the Sahara and there was also difficulty pumping the fuel out of the temporary float-tanks but while Cape Town was not made, the eventual landing on the Orange River off Alexander Bay – some 6,045 miles beyond the Tay – set a new record for the world's seaplane longest distance. That record stands to this day. *Picture from the collection of Richard Stenlake.*

The man who brought flying to the masses was Alan John Cobham (1894-1973). In 1926 he flew from London to Australia, a ground-breaking achievement for which he was awarded a knighthood. He was a pioneer of long distance flight, surveyed routes for Imperial Airways, and championed the interests of flying. He made sure that children and the young in general were given the opportunity to fly and operated a DH.61 which he named *Youth of Britain* to give free flights. He championed the cause of regional airports, emphasising the need for every town of even average size to have its own airport. As a director of Airspeed Ltd, he put the company on the map by having it produce its first proper aeroplane – the Airspeed Ferry – two of which he subsequently operated in his joy-riding displays. Above all he is mistakenly remembered for his 'Cobham's Flying Circus' – something that never was. What he did found in 1932 was his National Aviation Day displays all over the country. This also being the era of the barnstorming 'flying circuses', the misunderstanding is excusable. The inventor of a practical system of flight refuelling, after the end of the war he founded a company, later run by his son Michael John Cobham (1927-2006) at Tarrant Rushton. I was privileged to know both men in my own flying career.

Sir Alan Cobham was a master at promotion and he made sure that his National Air Days Displays were talked about. Everybody who went for a joy-ride was given a picture postcard to send to friend or family. This bore a picture of the aeroplane, the pilot – and a 'hand-written' message printed on it. Psychologically, the wording was masterful! 'As a flyer yourself you've liked it – Tell others. Alan J Cobham'. This is one put out in 1934 and shows the portrait of Earl Bateman Fielden, the 35-year-old chairman, managing director and chief pilot to Aviation Tours Ltd. He had been with Berkshire Aviation Tours and Surrey Aviation Services. The card also promoted Aerofilms Ltd and was stamped on the reverse 'Sign the Mandate for British Aviation'. *Picture from the collection of Richard Stenlake.*

The story behind the Airspeed Ferry 'miniature airliner' is strange because it would not have been made had it not been for the disaster that befell the R.101 airship. Britain was engaged in making two airships, the other being the R.100 built by the Airship Guarantee Company, a subsidiary of Vickers. After the tragedy, the government abandoned the whole programme and ordered the scrapping of the provenly-successful sister airship – the R.100 – which had already flown to Canada and back. The design staff were thrown out of work so several of them got together to form their own company which they called Airspeed Ltd and set up on March 13th 1931. Under-funded and based in a one-time York bus garage, the new firm had among its directors Lord Grimthorpe (later to sponsor North Eastern Airways which would connect London with Edinburgh, Perth and Dundee) and Sir Alan Cobham the long distance pilot and founder of the National Aviation Day displays, later popularly if incorrectly remembered as Cobham's Flying Circus. The designer was Alfred Hessell Tiltman (1891-1975) and stressman-cum-salesman Neville Shute Norway who would make a name for himself as an acclaimed novelist. They began by building a glider but Cobham saw the business as an opportunity to make an aircraft suited to his air display's passenger-carrying needs. The Ferry was the answer and after ten months the prototype, pictured here, was ready in its bus-depôt factory. To test-fly it at nearby Sherburn-in-Elmet Aerodrome meant towing the dismantled aircraft through the streets at dead of night. Still 16 feet wide, the cavalcade left with a police escort. All went well until 2.00 am near Tadcaster when the convoy came across the enormous rudder of the steamship *Berengaria* being towed with its own police escort in the opposite direction! Despite the ensuing chaos, the airport was reached at dawn and after assembly the aircraft was test-flown on April 5th, 1932. The selling price was £5,195 apiece and Cobham had two – this one and G-ABSJ. Two others were built for Midland & Scottish Air Ferries, a business run by John Sword who was a director and western manager for Scottish Motor Traction.

Cobham's National Air Day publicity ran to specially-taken pictures of his pilots posing with their aircraft. After passengers alighted from their joy-ride they could usually be induced to part with a further sixpence or so for a memento of their experience. Here is a postcard signed in 1934 by one such pilot, 29-year-old Charles William Henry Bebb, with his Gipsy Moth.
Picture from the collection of Richard Stenlake.

Those who were in at the beginning of aviation established links that spread far and wide throughout the industry as it grew. No better example of this can be found than the story of Aerofilms Ltd, a business started at Hendon in 1919 by pioneer aviator Claude Grahame-White and Francis Wills. The simple idea of taking pictures from the air formed the basis of a company that lasted well into modern times. Initially based at Stag Lane Aerodrome, first home of de Havilland, Aerofilms chartered AirCo DH.9 aircraft. Their pilot was one Alan Cobham. Years later, when Cobham had established his National Aviation Day displays, and Aerofilms had prestigious premises in London's Bush House (the then home to BBC World Service and other top companies between the Strand and Aldwych), it was not surprising that Aerofilms should be nominated as 'official photographers' and carry Cobham's promotional message 'sign the Mandate for British Aviation'. *Picture from the collection of Richard Stenlake.*

There's an amusing story associated with Sir Alan Cobham's Airspeed Ferry designed by A H Tiltman and Neville Shute Norway. Cobham needed a medium-capacity joy-riding aircraft to join his newly-founded National Aviation Day Displays for the summer of 1932. Engine availability and the need for propeller clearance directed that power would be provided by two de Havilland Gipsy II engines and one inverted Gipsy III, each offering 120 hp. The 10-seater Ferry was an enormous success and the prototype, G-ABSI seen here, made its first flight on April 21st, 1932, in the hands of Airspeed's test pilot 44-year-old Henry Vernon Worrall. The boy in this picture is the son of a man who witnessed BlŽriot's arrival from his cross-channel flight. This aircraft was a frequent visitor to Scotland with Cobham's air displays. Back in those days, 'officialdom' was only just starting to rear its ugly head and it was towards the Ferry that it chose to act. Because it carried ten people, it was officially classed as an airliner and when the Air Navigation Act demanded that all aircraft carrying ten and more passengers must carry radio, it was pointed out that the Ferry must carry wireless. There was a problem. Due to the sheer size and weight of the radio equipment then available, one passenger seat would have to be sacrificed, rendering the aircraft a nine-seater and thereby not required to carry wireless! After much negotiation commonsense prevailed: the Ferry never carried wireless equipment.

A famous name from the past – Kolster Brande – provided one of the public address systems for Sir Alan Cobham's National Aviation Day Displays. Although American-owned, KB was a British maker of radio receivers based at Foots Cray, Sidcup, Kent. While Tannoy became the name that everybody remembers today, KB was a close runner-up in the 1930s and this mobile PA-system complete with its drop-down front flap advertising Exide batteries, was a feature of Cobham's 1932-33 season in Scotland. The van also provided demonstrations of the company's radio receivers. It is seen here parked next to Cobham's triple-engined Airspeed Ferry. KB earned an international name for its wares after it negotiated a major contract to provide Cunard's passenger liners with communications systems. In 1938 it became part of what would be the empire of TV makers ITT at the Foots Cray premises. *Picture from the collection of Richard Stenlake.*

British Prime Minister Ramsay MacDonald (1866-1937) was not the most photogenic Scot of his era but historians recall him as one of the founders of the Labour Party and its first leader. He held the office of Prime Minister of the National Government from 1931 to 1936 but during this time his health deteriorated rapidly. He is pictured here on August 3rd, 1935, at Hatfield Aerodrome, the Hertfordshire home of the de Havilland Aircraft Company. Left is his daughter, Sheila and their pet dog 'Mr Jock', while to the right are Derwent Hall-Caine with Miss Peggy Naismith. Three of them are about to board Hall-Caine's DH.85 Leopard Moth, G-ACHC, to fly to Lossiemouth (Ramsay MacDonald's home) for the August Bank Holiday. Hall-Caine, one-time film-actor and political activist, was the second son of novelist Sir Thomas Henry Hall-Caine (1853-1931) and would go on to establish the Isle of Man's Hall-Caine Airport with his brother Ralph and, later that year, collect first a Knighthood and, two years later, a baronetcy. In November the following year, the then-ousted PM would be dead. As for the Leopard Moth, first registered on June 14th, 1933, it was impressed in August 1940 as BD167 and written off early in 1942. Hall-Caine Airport closed in 1939.

So far we have been looking at British-made aircraft. There was, though, the occasional exception and this is one. The Fokker F.XXII was a Dutch-designed and built airliner capable of carrying 22 passengers and powered by four 525 h.p. Pratt & Whitney Wasp radials. Four were built and two of these eventually ended up with Scottish Aviation Ltd at Prestwick in October 1939 having been purchased at the outbreak of war from KLM. The first, G-AFXR (PH-AJR), was impressed as HM159 and, on July 3rd, 1943, crashed into Loch Tarbert on the west side of Kintyre, Argyll, and exploded. The second, pictured here at Prestwick in February 1947, was G-AFZP (PH-AJP). This was operated by Scottish Airlines but by this time it was obsolete as compared with the faster and cheaper-to-run Douglas Dakotas SAL was converting. The old Fokker was withdrawn from use at Prestwick on August 10th 1947 and eventually broken up in July 1952. *Picture by E J Riding from the collection of Richard T Riding.*

The wide-open expanse of sea adds an extra dimension to the perils of communication by air, especially in time of war. This is a Royal Air Force Dominie (the Service name of the Dragon Rapide) of Transport Command pictured sometime in 1942 leaving the rugged shore of the West Coast en route to the Outer Hebrides. During the war, when private flying was prohibited and civil flying and airline activity heavily restricted, communication flights maintained a skeleton service mainly for Service personnel and essential business. Throughout the war years, aircraft passenger windows had to be blacked out so it was impossible to look out of the cabin. The reasoning behind this remains as uncertain today as it was then, especially since cameras were also prohibited.

De Havilland DH.86B G-AENR of Railway Air Services had a curious history and a very short Impressment as a military aircraft. First registered on February 8th, 1937, it served with West Coast Air Services Ltd for two years before going to Guernsey Airways Ltd in Jersey. Just in time to avoid the German Occupation of the Channel Islands, it was recalled in July 1940 and impressed for the Royal Navy as AX842. Just a month later it was restored to Railway Air Services and was employed on the West Coast routes through to Renfrew. In this picture it is seen in war time civilian markings with the registration underscored in red, white and blue and a Service-type flash on its 'Zulu-shield' finlets. One of only three of these handsome four-engined DH biplanes to survive the war, it was scrapped at Langley in November, 1948. *Picture by George A Cull.*

Prestwick Airport's story is one of seemingly endless struggle for survival in port-war aviation. As well as Scottish Aviation Ltd's almost perpetual fight to survive, the airport had its own chain of crises. Developed through the untiring efforts of David F McIntyre and the Marquis of Clydesdale, Douglas Douglas-Hamilton – they had together made the first-ever flight over Mount Everest in April, 1933 – the land had originally been a Royal Flying Corps landing ground named Monkton after the close-by village. It enjoyed a special location that meant it was flyable almost every day of the year thanks to a meteorological quirk that kept the bad weather at bay. Despite its ideal location, well into modern times, Prestwick Airport has had to battle for its very existence. In post-war years, the airport became the essential intermediate stop for transatlantic flights and, until the development of more fuel-efficient aircraft, aircraft bound for North America from not just London but elsewhere in Europe, would stop there for refuelling. At this time the airport printed special postcards that were given to travellers to send around the world promoting Prestwick Airport. Here is one posted at the airport on June 14th, 1952.

An amazing booklet, now extremely rare, was published in June 1944 by The Ayrshire Post Ltd. With no author's name but bearing all the signs of being from the prolific brain of Scottish Aviation's David Fowler McIntyre (it includes a picture of him with Thomas Johnston, MP and Secretary of State for Scotland at a Prestwick Aerodrome dinner on November 29th 1943 – the third anniversary of the transatlantic air link), the 16-page content is an unrestrained statement of the state of British aviation. No panegyric this, however, for it is an outspoken assessment of what the author saw as the need for post-war strategic planning. The prose, verging on the vitriolic, would have done credit to Charles Grey Grey, the forthright editor of *The Aeroplane.*

Featured inside the 18-page booklet *Transport Tomorrow*, as well as being drawn on the cover, is a photograph of the extraordinary twin-fuselaged six-engined airliner that Scottish Aviation 'registered' in 1943 and 'scheduled for production very early in the post-war years'. With a range sufficient for the longest ocean crossings the load capacity offered 100 passengers and 27,000 lbs of freight on stages of 4,000 miles, or 160 passengers and 69,000 lbs of freight on 1,500-mile stages the whole having an all-up weight of 300,000 lbs and tare weight of 154,600 lbs. The shape of the aircraft was intentional so that both landplane and flying-boat variants could be created from the same airframe. Of course, it never happened. Clearly the brainchild of David F McIntyre, in a moment of astute prescience, he called his aircraft 'Concord'.

Proving something about 'beggars not being able to be choosers', the shortage of suitable aircraft to operate UK services at the end of the war, we were quick to spot that the Junkers Ju.52/3m with its delightfully quirky corrugated external metalwork would make as rugged a workhorse for us as it did for the Luftwaffe. A dozen were 'liberated' as part of war reparations and converted by Short Brothers & Harland at Belfast for use by Railway Air Services and then BEA on internal services. With its propensity for naming everything, BEA called them 'Jupiters' and operated them on the Northolt – Renfrew service also flying to Prestwick and, occasionally, Turnhouse. G-AHOK was one of these and on January 26th, 1947, it was damaged beyond repair in a heavy landing at Renfrew where it was pictured dismantled the following month. This mishap was the beginning of the end for the Jupiters and they were all withdrawn the following month for breaking up at Warrington in 1948. They had nevertheless served as important stop-gap utility aircraft and had been popular with their pilots who found them heavy but otherwise pleasant to fly. *Picture by E J Riding from the collection of Richard T Riding.*

During the war, Scottish Aviation Ltd had undertaken a number of passenger conversions of aircraft, mostly Liberators and Dakotas, as executive-style transports. The former made a deluxe 24-seat civil airliner and a number was converted for use by Scottish Airlines. The biggest opportunity, though, lay with the C-47 or Dakota and SAL was able to offer a choice between a 21 seat airliner (deluxe or standard) and a corporate conversion for 'business executives and private owners'. The surplus aircraft came from the United States War Assets Administration and its storage base at Silloth on the Solway Firth – half an hour's flying time from Prestwick. Some of these aircraft were acquired at a token price of one dollar apiece. SAL quoted a variety of conversion packages with an attractive delivery time of between six and ten weeks depending on the customer's specification. Orders flooded in from all over Europe and Scandinavia. SAL had already worked very closely with the American Douglas company during the war and now obtained an official licence to represent the company in the UK. Similar negotiations followed with engine makers Pratt & Whitney. In 1950, British European Airways (BEA) ordered 38 aircraft equipped as 32-seaters. They wanted to call them 'Pioneer' class but David McIntyre already had reserved this name for his Prestwick Pioneer so BEA grudgingly accepted as an alternative the name 'Pionair'. It was Pionairs that served on not just all BEA's Scottish routes but most of its European services. Here one sits at Grimsetter while service vehicles (including a bus for the passengers) attend to its needs. *Picture from the collection of Richard Stenlake.*

Among the many aircraft which Scottish Aviation Ltd converted to civilian airliner configuration at Prestwick was the Consolidated-Vultee Liberator II. This was an amazingly versatile aircraft although as regards passenger comfort the conversion was very much a compromise. Several were used for freighting and one established something of a record on May 7th, 1948, when it transported a ship's propeller shaft weighing six tons seven hundredweight (6,452 kilogrammes) and measuring nineteen feet six inches in length from Prestwick to Calcutta. The Glasgow-based Clan Line shipping company had been founded by Sir Charles William Cayzer (1843-1916) and David McIntyre was asked to assist when the SS *Clan Angus* suffered a prop-shaft failure in the Bay of Bengal. Scottish Airlines (Prestwick) Ltd operated G-AGZI as a long-range transport. Originally marked as AL557, it served from September 1946 until February 1948 when it was sold to Hellenic Airlines, Athens, as SX-DAA. *Picture from the Richard Riding Collection.*

Another of the long-nosed Liberator II conversions was G-AHZP (AL516) which gained its C of A on August 12th 1946 and lasted until October 13th 1948 when it crashed on landing at Speke (Liverpool), fortunately without loss of life or serious injury. It undershot the runway and collided with two street lamps adjacent to the airport. At the time of its loss it had been wet-leased to Iceland Airways and was operating a cargo flight en route to Reykjavik. *Picture by E J Riding from the collection of Richard T Riding.*

If the DC-3 was the monoplane workhorse of the immediate post-war years, then the de Havilland DH.89 and DH.89a Dragon Rapide were the biplane equivalents. The skies were a-buzz with these nippy craft which had a distinctive sound – a combination of a pair of Gipsy Six engines and the Aeolian harp effect of the multiple bracing wires. Occasionally its big sister, the DH.86, would appear but at the end of the war only three of these four-engined biplanes which were essentially a scaled-up version of the 89a survived. Pictured at Renfrew in May 1946, G-AFRK had first been registered on March 9th, 1939, and had managed to remain in civil markings throughout the war. In March 1959, on the expiry of its C of A, this aircraft was broken up at far-off Christchurch in Hampshire. *Picture by E J Riding from the collection of Richard T Riding.*

Railway Air Services operated its fleet of DC-3 aircraft around Scotland from Renfrew where this picture was taken early in 1947. G-AGZB (FZ624) first flew in civil marks on February 21st 1946. By 1962 it was owned by Channel Airways. On May 6th that year it was flying from Jersey to Portsmouth in poor weather. It struck the top of St Boniface Down at Ventnor, Isle of Wight, killing twelve of the eighteen on board. The accident was attributed to pilot error and by coincidence the present author was technical consultant to the subsequent enquiry. *Picture by E J Riding from the collection of Richard T Riding.*

During its fifteen-year existence, Scottish Airlines Ltd was a major operator in the post-war skies. The workhorses were the Rapides and the Dakotas or DC-3 as they were properly called in civilian life. G-AGWS (WZ984) was an early conversion to civilian use and gained its C of A on December 28th 1945. This picture reveals one of the aircraft's advantages – the huge access door through which large items of cargo could be inserted as well as passengers and their baggage. These were also the days of rather primitive access steps up and down which passengers had to be steadied by the cabin crew. This view shows what looks like hay-bales in the foreground which is unlikely since cylindrical balers were not available in Britain at this time until the introduction of Vermeer patent balers after 1947. They are more likely to be tie-down blocks made of concrete that can be rolled into position. In July 1952, G-AGWS went to Canada as CF-FCQ. *Picture from the Richard Riding Collection.*

From the foregoing it can be understood that British airlines could not have started up so quickly after the war had it not been for the availability of surplus military aircraft converted for passenger-carrying. Scottish Aviation Ltd's Prestwick factory quickly became world-renowned specialists in this work. For the Dakota, it called for the removal of the navigator's compartment to provide luggage space, replacing the metal cabin floor with a sound and vibration damping balsa-wood laminate, sound-proofing the whole interior, fitting a carpeted floor and upholstered plywood cabin lining including lighting, luggage-racks, passenger call-buttons, personal ventilation ducting, ash-trays, hand-rails and finally adjustable upholstered seats. Here is one of BEA's so-called Pionairs, G-AJIC registered on February 18th, 1947. After a long and rich career it was last seen derelict behind a hangar at far-off Benina Airport in Libya during August, 1966. *Picture from the collection of Richard Stenlake.*

It is February of 1947 at Renfrew as passengers board DC-3 G-AIOE for the service down to London. In those far-off days, London was served by five airports. Croydon was still open but would soon close, Heston was still open but was about to close before the M4 motorway would obliterate it and Hanworth Air Park was about to shut forever due to its proximity to the newly-built Heathrow. Heathrow was gradually drawing the airlines away from what had been London's prime airport at the restart of commercial flying in 1945 – Northolt. The only real drawback to Northolt as London's airport was that of communication as it lay two miles from Uxbridge and six miles north of the new Heathrow. It is hard to realise that in 1946-7 this was the busiest airport in Europe and was the base for BEA and its many operations. And, unlike Prestwick, nobody thought to give it a rail link! *Picture by E J Riding from the collection of Richard T Riding.*

Scottish Airlines (Prestwick) Ltd was set up in 1946 as a wholly-owned subsidiary of Scottish Aviation Ltd. The airline flourished until the era of the Civil Aviation (Licensing) Bill in February 1960 which saw the need to have a central administration to handle licensed for airline operations and their routes. With BEA champing at its heels, these were bleak days for independence in aviation. Scottish Airlines ceased operations that November and the following year its routes and aircraft were acquired by Dan-Air. DC-3 G-AIOF, pictured here at Renfrew in February of 1948, operated a regular service from Prestwick to London (Northolt) via Burtonwood. This was challenged by BEA which operated its Vickers Viscounts on its direct 'Clansman' service from Northolt to Renfrew – besides being direct it was far quicker and the turboprop Viscount scored over the DC-3 in terms of cabin noise levels. *Picture by E J Riding from the collection of Richard T Riding.*

A Royal Air Force Vickers Varsity makes a low pass at Glasgow's Renfrew Airport. So close was Renfrew to Abbotsinch that the circuits virtually overlapped. Originally the site was known as Moorpark Airfield.

The Flying Flea craze of the mid-1930s was the result of Frenchman Henri Mignet's design of 'everyman's aeroplane' – the *Pou-du-Ciel.* Promoted enthusiastically by its designer as the aircraft anybody could make, the craze spread through France and into Britain. At Dyce, 20-year-old James Goodall was one of the many UK enthusiasts who eagerly built an example. His Flea, G-ADXY, was powered by a Scott Flying Squirrel engine and by some cunning subterfuge he got Aberdeen Airways' John Neilan to test-fly it for him on March 13th, 1936. Neilan reported glowingly on the machine's performance. Goodall flew his aircraft around Dyce with the glee of the successful home-builder. He was enjoying himself, flying well and presumably having fun. But then he ran out of petrol and the engine stopped. The aircraft came down gently but ran into a ditch. The pilot, not strapped in, was flung forward and killed. At the inquest (at which Neilan gave evidence) it was revealed that poor James Goodall had never had a flying lesson in his life but had taught himself how to fly in his Flea. His aeroplane, sound though it had proven itself to be, had no airworthiness certification or Permit to Fly and had not even been checked over by a licensed engineer. John Neilan was as surprised as everybody else to find he had test-flown an unchecked aircraft. History has since implied that the Flying Flea (which was, unfortunately, unstable if the C of G moved only a minute distance from the optimum) was a killer and was banned. In fact it killed three people through in-flight lack of control with the result that further building and flying was discouraged, not banned. James Goodall was not one of the Flea's victims, though, for he was killed through his absence of flying training preventing him from knowing how to cope with engine failure and a forced landing and exacerbated by not wearing a safety harness. Scotland had another Flea builder – the renowned Dr Matthew David Sutherland Armour of Anstruther who was a world authority on his main work – budgerigar-breeding.

Montrose around the time of the outbreak of the Second World War. It is hard to believe but we still had biplanes in front-line fighter squadrons when it all started. Small wonder the better equipped Luftwaffe led the Third Reich to consider that Britain would be a push-over in an invasion. Even so, here are some of 603 Squadron's Hawker Hart and Hind fighters pictured in 1936. *Picture from the collection of Richard Stenlake.*

At Montrose Aerodrome in 1936 one of the resident 603 Squadron's Kestrel-powered Hawker Hart aircraft is being prepared for flight. Despite the sighting of a Bessoneaux hangar between the aircraft's post wings, note the otherwise permanent hangars and a greater air of an established air base than seen in the First World War era views. *Picture from the collection of Richard Stenlake.*

The Naval Construction Works at Dalmuir was home to William Beardmore & Co Ltd and during the First World War the company manufactured huge numbers of fighter aircraft for the RFC and fledgling RAF. In went on to distinguish itself in the famous Light Aeroplane Trials on the early 1920s but then, seeking something to keep it heavily engaged in aviation work, it acquired the rights to the German patented method of construction devised by Adolf Karl Rohrbach (1889-1939) and embarked on a vast metal monoplane that it named the Inflexible. Designed between 1925 and 1927, this metal giant had a wingspan some 15 feet greater than a WWII Boeing B-29 bomber. It made its first flight on March 5th, 1928, but was hopelessly underpowered and overweight. With three Rolls-Royce Condor engines each of 650 hp, it would just touch 109 mph if pushed. A heavy and impractical aircraft, the Beardmore Inflexible was ugly and eschewed a crude primitiveness that rather negated the tremendous step forward that its structure represented for it was one of the first all-metal stressed-skin aircraft. The twenty-ton aircraft was said to be too big for most airfields but managed to land at RAF Hendon for the Air Display on September 7th 1928 where it demonstrated its brick-like gliding angle. But nobody wanted the 157 feet 6 inches wing span monster. Pensioned out in the open as a test piece for metal corrosion, the Inflexible was another of the many pointless byways thought to lead to aviation supremacy. The Great Depression following the Wall Street Crash followed and the decision to shut down Beardmore's aviation division became unavoidable. The Inflexible marked the end of the old firm's hitherto distinguished part in aviation history.

David Kay's first Gyroplane, known simply as the Type 32/1, was first flown at Scone before being transferred to the RAF aerodrome at Leuchars in Fife in 1932. Here it underwent numerous trial flights. The engine was a 40 hp ABC Scorpion flat twin. After a number of successful flights including some by experienced RAF pilots, it was damaged in an accident in 1933 and was not repaired. This machine never carried a civil registration. Kay worked quite independently of both Juan de la Cierva and fellow Scot James Weir at Cathcart.

Kay's second Gyroplane was styled the Type 33/1 and built for him by Oddie, Bradbury & Cull Ltd at Eastleigh. This company specialised in Autogiro sub-contract work and their forte was in making rotor blades. Seen here in its original form, G-ACVA was powered by a 75 hp Pobjoy R radial. The coarse-pitch four-blade propeller was essential to absorb the engine power whilst keeping the overall diameter down to clear both ground and rotor. Rotor pre-spin was possible through an engine clutch and gear-box so that jump take-offs could be achieved. Here the machine is pictured just before its first flight on February 18th 1935.

Combining rotor tilting (side to side) with collective pitch, the Kay was technically ahead of Cierva from its inception although Cierva did later catch up and adopt the rudiments of Kay's control system. Here Arthur Rawson, seen in the cockpit, is discussing maiden flight tactics with Kay (right) and an unknown person standing the other side while the engine ticks over at low revs at Southampton's Eastleigh Aerodrome. The date was February 18th, 1935. The reasons for the Southampton first flight were first that it was close to Eastleigh where the machine had been built and, second. Arthur Rawson was one of the most experienced rotary-winged pilots of the time. Note how rigid the rotor blades appear.

There is something deeply saddening about an aircraft that has lived a life of vitality only to be confined for the rest of its days as a museum exhibit, silent and stared-at. Nevertheless better that than total oblivion. After its last flight at Perth's Scone Airport on August 16th, 1947, it was stored for many years. After renovation back at Scone in 1967, Kay's revolutionary Gyroplane was loaned to Glasgow's Museum of Transport. The National Museum of Scotland subsequently acquired the aircraft from the descendants of David Kay and today it is on display in the main museum building in Chambers Street, Edinburgh. Occasionally over the past decades it has appeared as a static exhibit at air shows where, thanks to incorrect and incomplete signing, generations of young and old walk past it without casting so much as a second look. Clearly they are unaware that this was a trend-setting and innovative design closer to today's helicopter than might be expected.

James Weir had supported Juan de la Cierva from the first, advising him to set up a British company and helping him to get started in Britain. Obtaining a licence from Cierva, Weir began developing his own series of Autogiros in Glasgow and embarked on a course that would ultimately lead away from the Autogiro to the creation of Britain's first successful helicopter. First came the Weir Autogiros. Although built at the Cathcart, Glasgow, factory, the 15-foot long Weir W-1 was taken by road to the Cierva Autogiro Company headquarters at Hanworth, Middlesex, where in May of 1933 it made its first flight in the hands of Henry Alan Marsh. The ply-covered monocoque fuselage mounted a triple-finned tail while the engine was the 40 hp Douglas Dryad. The two-blade rotor had a diameter of 28 feet. This quickly gave way to the W.2, similar but powered by a 45/50 hp 1,500 cc Weir flat-twin designed by former Douglas Dryad designers Cyril George Pullin and Michael Walker. A reduction gear turned a coarse-pitch prop at a relatively slow, efficient speed. It was also one of the earliest machines to be fitted with a silencer – a useful and necessary accessory with an open engine too close to a pilot's ears for comfort. It first flew at Abbotsinch in June 1934 before being taken to Hanworth where this picture was taken. In the background, left, can be seen the Klemm and BA hangars at Hanworth, later to be used by General Aircraft Ltd. The first flight took place at Hanworth.

Head-on view of the well-streamlined Weir W-2 pictured at Hanworth in 1934. Thanks to the involvement of Cyril George Pullin who brought with him the expertise of Douglas Engines, Weir was the only Autogiro company that actually made its own aircraft engines. This is a twin-cylinder motor based on the Douglas Dryad. Note the extremely small wheels which must have made for difficult ground handling on the grass at Hanworth but Weir obviously worked out that an Autogiro with a pre-rotator for spinning up the rotor didn't need to taxi about on the ground.

Here the two-blade Weir W-2 reveals its finely-crafted plywood monocoque fuselage and neat Weir engine which developed between 45 and 50 hp. Intended to be sold to the private owner for £355, projected production never materialised through insoluble teething problems mostly due to vibration and the aircraft was superseded by the W-3. Here Marsh boards for a test flight at Hanworth to try out the extra-large rotor pylon fairing just fitted.

From August 1934 comes this rare picture of the Weir W-2 Autogiro in flight over the Great West Road near Hanworth. The large amount of open countryside is noticeable. Today this is fully built over and beneath the aircraft would lie the sprawl of London's Heathrow Airport. Despite its designer's high hopes, the W-2 never quite lived up to expectations and in the end severe vibration could not be remedied and a below-par performance combined to justify abandoning development. Even so it notched up at least ten hours of test-flying. Surviving the war in storage, it was allowed a rare curtain-call as a static exhibit in the historic aircraft park at the *Daily Express* 'Fifty Years of Flying' exhibition at Hendon in 1953.

The W-3 arrives at Hanworth for erection. Note its small size and the neat, compact Weir Pixie in-line inverted four-cylinder engine designed by Pullin and another former Douglas designer, Michael Walker.

If David Kay's Gyroplane was small, by comparison with Cierva's machines at Hanworth, the Weir W-3 was tiny. Here engine designer Pullin poses for size in front of his creation. The Pixie was a clockwise tractor (when viewed from the front) and the ground clearance of the propeller blade tips was marginal.

This view shows the W-3's salient points including the over-large tail and the twin-blade rotor.

The triple-tailed Weir W-3 was a jump-start autogiro. It was fitted with a special two-blade rotor and powered by a Weir Pixie four-cylinder inverted in-line engine of 55 hp. The Pixie was for its time an amazing little motor weighing the magical two pounds per horse-power. Cierva's latest design of 'autodynamic' rotor head fitted with just two rotor blades made this a true 'state-of-the-art' machine. Design and construction began in 1935 and took six people just twelve months. Usurping (for the moment) the facilities of Hanworth and the Cierva factory, the first flight was made at Glasgow's Abbotsinch Airport on July 9th 1936 by 35-year-old Henry Alan Marsh. It was then loaded, fully assembled, onto a lorry and driven down to the Cierva works at Hanworth Air Park, to the west of London prior to demonstrations at Hounslow Heath (pictured here) on July 23rd and a public showing at the August Bank Holiday display at Brooklands. With ideas of marketing it, Weir quoted a retail price of £500 for the W-3 but it never entered production. Instead the company moved towards helicopters and the W-4. The W-3 did surprisingly little flying and was eventually 'reduced to produce' in the advance of other things.

The cockpit, pylon and rotor of the W-3. The hanging control-column is in the 'locked' position, secured by a catch at the bottom of the instrument panel. Above this is the fore-and-aft pivot trunnion and just above that is the ball-joint in the main rotor-control arm. Moving the stick from side to side rocks the pivot trunnion and operates cyclic pitch to turn or bank. Lower left of the cockpit is the throttle for the engine and above it the control to operate the clutch for the rotor spin-up, and the locking lever to secure the rotor blades in the 'feathered' position. The instrument panel shows, centrally, the bubble level, left a warning notice about minimum rotor speed for take-off, centrally (behind the control column) the engine tachometer, above right the rotor rpm indicator right of that (out of sight behind the cockpit coaming) the altimeter and beneath it, visible, the double Tiger Moth-type ignition switches. The heavy forward shaft centrally in front of the pylon is the drive to the rotor clutch. On top of the rotor can be seen the quadrant channels cast in magnesium alloy which guide the rotor pitch control lever followers.

An inherent problem with the Autogiro was the tendency to 'dance' on the ground and roll over to one side if taxied cross wind at near to take-off rotor speed. One way thought ideal to resist this aerodynamic characteristic was to have a wide-track undercarriage. The W-3 did not disappoint.

The W-3 in flight. Interestingly, the Spanish design of the Autogiro had considered that multiple rotor blades were preferable and, although he experimented with a C.30 having a two-bladed rotor, this was a short-lived trial and production models settled on three rotor blades. The Weir concept was to employ just two blades but it was found that much of the in-flight vibration problems were down to this format. In the end, the two-blade rotor, while elegant and simple, was never used other than experimentally.

From the Weir W-3 came the improved version described as the W-4 seen here at the works of G & J Weir Ltd, Cathcart, Glasgow, on December 21st 1937. Pixie-powered like the W-3 and with a streamlined rotor-pylon housing, it suffered catastrophic rotor imbalance and resonance problems, overturning at Abbotsinch during taxi trials. In the cockpit was Henry Marsh who had done most of the Weir Autogiro flying because he was easily able to fit into their small cockpits: Cierva and autogiro test pilot Reginald Brie expressed themselves as less than comfortable in the confined seats. After the accident, which happened shortly after this picture was taken, Weir's directors met on December 28th and voted to abandon Autogiro work and concentrate on helicopters. The Pixie-engined W-5 flew the following June.

Weir's chief designer Cyril George Pullin, originally believed it would be possible to convert the W-4 into a powered-rotor helicopter using co-axial rotors but in the end the W-5, pictured here, was designed and built as a twin-rotor machine, each rotor assembly carried on an outrigger rather like the successful Focke 61 which had already broken some records in Germany. Once again, though, two-blade rotors were used offering cyclic and collective pitch. Powered by the 50 hp Weir engine the fifteen-feet diameter rotors turned at 430 rpm. The photograph shows the aircraft in an advanced state of construction, together with its design staff. The designer's son, Raymond Aubrey Pullin, took the machine for its first flight at Dalrymple. It produced encouraging results and by the outbreak of war had notched up 80 flying hours and inspired the larger and more powerful W-6, the company's last rotary-wing project. The W-5 was Britain's first successful helicopter and its flight marked yet another 'first' for Scotland

Pictures of the Weir W-6 twin-rotor helicopter built at Cathcart in 1939 are extremely rare. Here are three factory shots taken during construction. Designed by Cyril George Pullin, the first twin-rotor machine had been the W-5 of 1937. The W-5 was a single-seater powered by a Weir Pixie, and it first flew at Dalrymple, Ayrshire, on June 7th, 1938. It was the success of this that inspired the larger W-6, design of which began in 1938.

With two seats and powered by a 205 hp de Havilland Gipsy Six inline engine, unlike the earlier Weir rotary-winged machines, this had three-bladed rotors each 25 feet in diameter. A ratchet-type freewheeling device was employed for flight in auto-rotation. Both rotors turned at 275 rpm and each had both cyclic and collective control enclosed within the hub.

The first flight of the W-6 took place at Argus Foundry, Thornliebank near Glasgow on October 27th, 1939, in the hands of Raymond A Pullin. The next day it carried pilot and two passengers – the first passenger helicopter flight in Britain. Some 70 flying hours were logged between then and July 1940 when the Weir Aviation Department was disbanded due to other war work.

The first original design and production aircraft to be made in Scotland was the Scottish Aviation Prestwick Pioneer. Here is an official Ministry of Supply photograph dated November 1947 showing the as-yet unmarked prototype powered by a Gipsy Queen six-cylinder in-line engine. Just visible on the fuselage is the white letter P in a circle next to the RAF roundels. Note also that the elevators are of the pre-production short-span type which do not extend beyond the span of the tailplane.

Service trials with the Prestwick Pioneer were extremely successful as well as being impressive. While pre-war aircraft taking part in the annual *Rundflug* have been pictured climbing at steeper angles than this to clear the mandatory boundary tape, their climbs were of brief duration and the stall was resisted by thrusting the nose down once the height had been reached. The Pioneer did not work that way. As it unstuck it simply went up at this angle – and stayed at that position as it steadily climbed! A triumph of STOL technology it was the nearest thing to true vertical take-off. The present author witnessed numerous demonstrations at, among others, RAF Hendon, where the aircraft crossed the high railway embankment and landed in the width of the perimeter track – a horizontal distance of about 60 yards. Note, incidentally, how much lower the elevator is than the tailwheel in this picture of XE515 – a quirk that resulted in an amazing demonstration at a SBAC Farnborough Show where the pilot pulled up so steeply he caught one elevator on the runway and partially pulled it off. He then safely completed a circuit with it dangling beneath the tailplane.

Prestwick Pioneer XE512 was demonstrated just about everywhere. One favourite trick of the demo pilot was to arrange an air-to-air photo shoot, as seen here, and then, while the photographer struggled with his camera – remember this was still the days of quite large, bulky photographic equipment – he would select flaps and slots and gradually slow down until either the camera plane disengaged and did a circuit or stalled and fell out of the sky. The camera pilot ought to have suspected something when he was told to formate at 8,000 feet – but he couldn't have known what was about to happen! In this fine shot, the cameraman was quick off the mark and got his picture. This aircraft was later registered G-AKBF.

The Prestwick Pioneer arrived in service in 1963 at the height of the Malaysian Emergency. The RAF was engaged in what was known as Operation Firedog and demonstrated the value of 'discretional air power' as having a major role in internal security operations. Although popular and easy to operate, the use of the Auster in Malaya was increasingly thwarted by the need to operate from ever smaller and rougher landing strips in conditions of high temperature and humidity. The Auster was limited to carrying just one passenger under these conditions and many were lost in accidents. The Pioneer was, consequently, a godsend to the operations. XJ466 was one of four Prestwick Pioneers shipped out to the Far East Air Force at the end of 1955 aboard the SS *Benwyvis*. Serving with 209 Squadron, it was severely damaged in a heavy landing at Ipoh, Perak, Malaysia, in November 1960 but was rebuilt at 389 Maintenance Unit and continued to serve until the end of 1964 when it was struck off charge. Other aircraft saw service with 78 Squadron at Khormakser, Aden, providing short range transport for Army units and the Aden Protectorate Levies in Southern Arabia. Later some were loaned to the Sultan of Oman's Air Force.

Three Scottish Aviation Pioneer CC.1 aircraft. Foreground is XL702 and centre XL703 coded X and Y and first flown November 30th 1956 and December 5th 1956 respectively. They saw service at Nicosia in Cyprus with 215 Squadron, subsequently renumbered as 230 squadron. The first of these machines survived until being struck off charge in January 1970 and dumped at RAF Tengah in the western part of Singapore. XL703 saw out its Service life and was pensioned off in January of 1969 for storage at the RAF Museum facility at Henlow. In the background of the picture is XL666 which first flew on October 2nd 1956. This machine was loaned back to Scottish Aviation Ltd for the 1957 SBAC Show at Farnborough. The aircraft also served with 230 Squadron and after a colourful life, including several quite severe mishaps and major rebuilds, it served with 209 squadron at Kuala Lumpur, eventually being struck off charge and abandoned at Tengah.

Pioneer XL704 served with the Far East Air Force sailing out aboard the SS *Doldus* and arriving on January 6th, 1959. It is seen here in a jungle clearing at an undisclosed hot and high location illustrating typical Pioneer operating country. Some of the airstrips used were so small and rough that they were extremely hard to see, being no more than a path through the jungle. The high attrition rate of the aircraft – 25 out of 40 squadron aircraft written off – was no reflection on the design but merely an indication of the appalling conditions under which the aircraft was operated. In November 1958, for example, 230 squadron's Pioneers flew a total of 1,350 hours making 4,130 landings of which 1,300 were on unprepared strips.

By 1955 there were some 72 airstrips throughout Malaya and the Pioneer had resoundingly demonstrated its ability at them all. Other types including Auster and Beaver had been used but could not match the Pioneer's STOL capabilities. If there were to be a leitmotif for jungle flying, then it would have been the Ayrshire-built marvel. Aircraft were shipped out on cargo vessels to Singapore, transported to the RAF Maintenance Base at Seletar (later to be known as 389/390 MU) and there assembled and flown. Each aircraft endured a rough, tough life and by 1957 the cumulative effect of more than 1,000 landings a year on each aircraft was begging to show. Rough and semi-prepared landing sites had taken their toll on the airframes and even the Pioneer's rugged character could not stand such continuous punishment. As serviceability fell it was clear that since the Pioneer had no equal, they must be refurbished. Work went ahead at Seletar to reinforce the aircraft for a further tour of duty. These modifications involved structural stiffening and beefing-up which extended the service life but placed a limitation on the maximum permitted take-off weight. XL706, seen here, was the last of a batch of aircraft that served with 267 squadron and it survived until the middle of 1968. The Pioneer had seen out the Malaysian campaign.

Developed from the Pioneer was a twin-engined version. The prototype Twin Pioneer, G-ANTP with its highly-polished bare metal finish, was first flown at Prestwick on June 25th, 1955, and shortly afterwards it was demonstrated at that year's Farnborough Air Show flown by Captain Roy Smith. Visible in this picture are the original ailerons which extended to the wing tips. Later examples had a full-chord wing tip fairing and the ailerons stopped short of the tips.

The prototype Twin Pioneer takes off for a demonstration flight. Originally the leading edge slats continued with a section inboard of the engines but early trials showed that these portions contributed little or nothing to the performance while adding complexity and weight so they were dispensed with.

Twenty-four propeller blades and a dozen fins and rudders practising formation-flying as four Twin Pioneers shuffle into some sort of order for the photographer's camera above a miserably even cloud cover somewhere over South Ayrshire.

Of the total of 87 Twin Pioneers manufactured at Prestwick, nineteen were originally for the British Civil register. This example, OE-BHV is a Series III and was registered on November 17th 1965 to the Austrian government.

The Twin Pioneer, like its single-engined predecessor, became something of a Jack of all Trades and the fourth aircraft built was used by the Rio Tinto Finance & Exploration Company in 1959 for geophysical surveying. Used to explore 19,300 square miles of Mexico and Lower California between 1962 and 1963, it was equipped with the highly sensitive airborne magnetometer surveying equipment and receiving coils in wing tip containers. G-AOER is pictured here at Prestwick just prior to delivery.

Scottish Aviation Twin Pioneer Srs.3 (two 640 hp Alvis Leonides 531 engines) G-APRS first flew in September 1959 and was operated by British United Airways before passing to the Empire Test Pilots' School at Farnborough in March 1965. Allocated the serial XT610, it is seen here in the unusual livery of a Service aircraft with civil markings.

The Prestwick-built Scottish Aviation Bulldog began life at the other end of the British Isles as a design by the failed Beagle company at Shoreham on the Sussex coast. SAL took over the entire design and, importantly, the useful order book from the bankrupt business and successfully put it into production. XX628 is one of a large batch built for the Royal Air Force.

The Scottish Aviation Bulldog enjoyed a long and fulfilling Service life as a trainer to replace the ageing DHC-1 Chipmunk. Here XX669 is pictured at RAF Shawbury, Shropshire, in March 1977. Operated by the University of Birmingham Air Squadron, it entered service the previous June and was a popular and capable trainer.

A wide cockpit offering side-by-side seating provided the ideal environment for pilot training. The days of tandem seating, which were perpetuated by the Moth and sustained by Magister and Chipmunk, were consigned to oblivion as pilot and instructor could communicate easily and also, crucially, watch what each was doing! This would be sustained into the next generation of ad ignition trainers such as the Grob and Provost before extending into pure-jet trainers such as the Jet Provost.

The Bulldog's many merits included easy cockpit entry and exit via a large sliding canopy which contributed to excellent all-round visibility - essentials for proper flying training. The small fin-like protrusion on the fuselage top just aft of the sliding canopy is the radio aerial enclosure.

Handley Page Ltd had its works in Cricklewood, North London, which was once also the company airfield back in the 1920s but is now heavily built up. The business also developed Radlett Aerodrome in Hertfordshire. The company's hey-day was the war time production of Halifax bombers but as the 1950s approached, founder Sir Frederick Handley Page was totally opposed to the policy of company mergers and acquisitions that had begun in 1935 with the formation of Hawker Siddeley. Believing that his independence was essential and his company future thus secure, he ignored the fact that aircraft development was now a high-cost process that demanded larger organisations and fewer participants. After the Victor V-bomber, he built the four-engined Herald – obsolete before it ever flew. The twin turboprop version was successful but made for a compromise airframe. The company then conceived the idea of making a small turboprop transport aimed at world third level and executive markets. The outcome was the Jetstream but once more the company chose the wrong engines, certainly as far as the American market was concerned. The French Turboméca Astazou XIV 840 ehp engines, seen in this picture, did not go down well there. Passenger capacity was up to eighteen although the executive version carried just ten seats. Meanwhile Scottish Aviation Ltd had netted a lucrative contract to build the wings for Handley Page. Unfortunately, HP needed bread and butter work meaning military contracts and these were not forthcoming. Sir Frederick and his policies did not fit in with the establishment. Work dwindled while Jetstream orders increased. Without sufficient operating cash the company went into receivership leaving SAL with unpaid work and a lot of wings. After several false sunrises, SAL bit the bullet and bought the whole project from the receiver. Production and development at Prestwick eventually saw the replacement of the Astazou with the American Garrett AiResearch TPE-331 series engines of 904 ehp. While the design had been hampered from inception by grossly excess airframe weight, SAL (now known as the Scottish division of BAe) set about revamping the Radlett jet and in 1989 launched the new 29-seater Jetstream 41. This picture shows the HP-built prototype of 1967 – a heavyweight baby with an unwise choice of engines.

Handley Page Ltd had gone into liquidation on February 27th, 1970, victim of numerous circumstances, not all of outside origin. This pioneering company's last design had been the HP.137 Jetstream and the prototype, G-AWBR, seen here, made its first flight on November 21st, 1968. The design was a moderate success but needed development in the face of interest from around the world. As the once-great HP company folded, the future of the Jetstream was virtually non-existent until Scottish Aviation Ltd, already under contract to build the wing panels, saw an opportunity to take over the whole design and development project from the receivers. The outcome was a whole range of Jetstream variants from Prestwick. As for G-AWBR it was scrapped at Radlett in 1970 as the company went under.

The name Highland Airways was revived with a brand new company in 1991. Based in Inverness it was developed from a flying school operation called Air Alba. The new incarnation operated to the Western Islands (Inner and Outer Hebrides), Oban and Inverness as well as routes to Cardiff and Anglesey using ten Scottish Aviation Jetstreams and one Britten-Norman Islander. Here one of the Jetstream aircraft, G-ATXG, poses on the apron at Benbecula Airport. All was not well, however, and in March 2010 Highland Airways went into receivership with the loss of many jobs.

Two Scottish Aviation Jetstream aircraft of the Royal Navy. Nearest the camera is XX478, built at Prestwick as a T.2 for the RN. The other aircraft, ZA110, was originally built at Radlett as a T.1 for France as F-BTMI. It then went to Zaire as 9Q-CTC before being acquired for the Navy whereupon it brought up to T.2 standard at Prestwick.

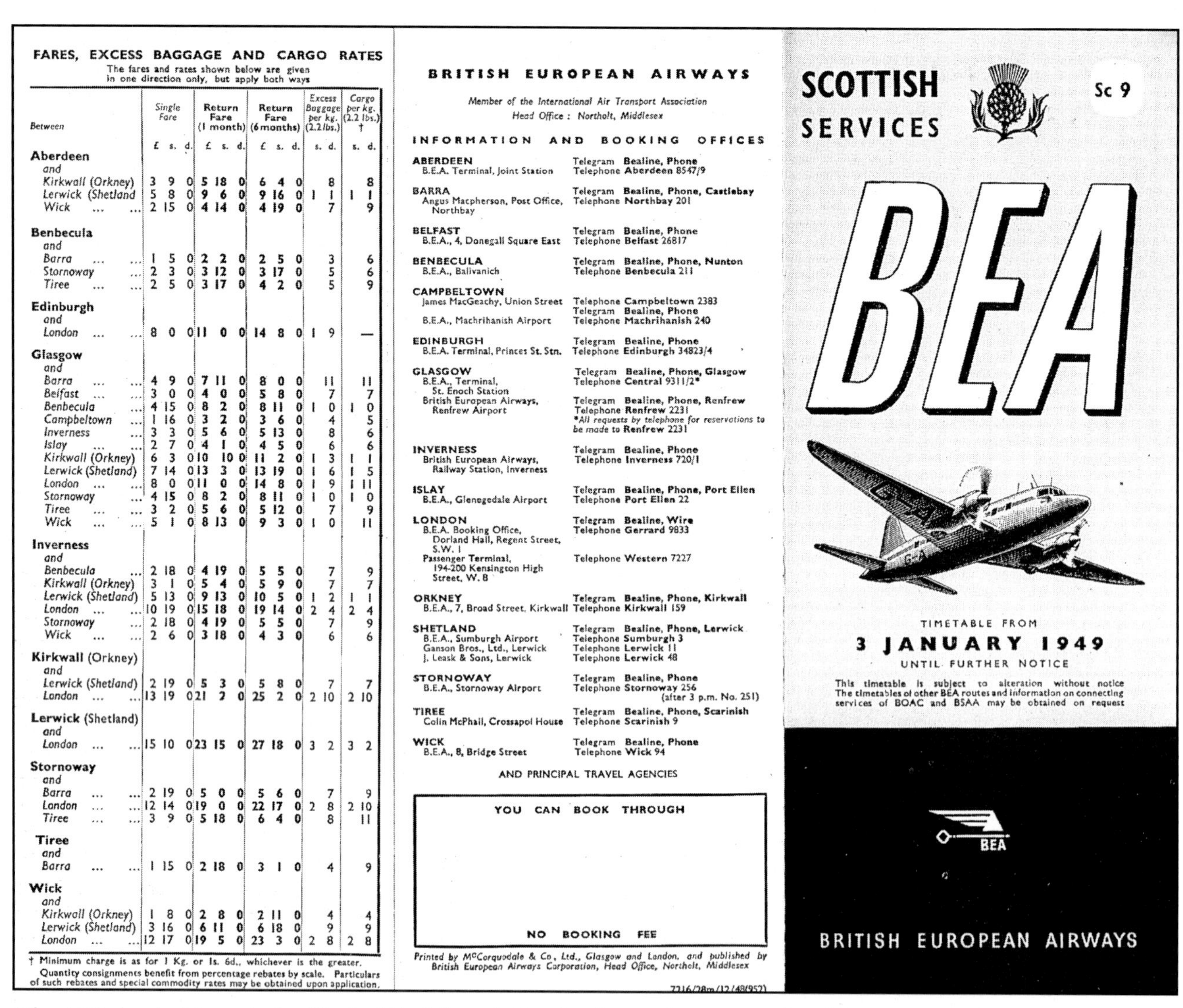

FARES, EXCESS BAGGAGE AND CARGO RATES

The fares and rates shown below are given in one direction only, but apply both ways

Between	Single Fare £	s.	d.	Return Fare (1 month) £	s.	d.	Return Fare (6 months) £	s.	d.	Excess Baggage per kg. (2.2 lbs.) s.	d.	Cargo per kg. (2.2 lbs.) † s.	d.
Aberdeen and													
Kirkwall (Orkney)	3	9	0	5	18	0	6	4	0		8		8
Lerwick (Shetland	5	8	0	9	6	0	9	16	0	1	1	1	1
Wick	2	15	0	4	14	0	4	19	0		7		9
Benbecula and													
Barra	1	5	0	2	2	0	2	5	0		3		6
Stornoway ...	2	3	0	3	12	0	3	17	0		5		6
Tiree	2	5	0	3	17	0	4	2	0		5		9
Edinburgh and													
London	8	0	0	11	0	0	14	8	0	1	9		—
Glasgow and													
Barra	4	9	0	7	11	0	8	0	0		11		11
Belfast	3	0	0	4	0	0	5	8	0		7		7
Benbecula ...	4	15	0	8	2	0	8	11	0	1	0	1	0
Campbeltown ...	1	16	0	3	2	0	3	6	0		4		5
Inverness ...	3	3	0	5	6	0	5	13	0		8		6
Islay	2	7	0	4	1	0	4	5	0		6		6
Kirkwall (Orkney)	6	3	0	10	10	0	11	2	0	1	3	1	1
Lerwick (Shetland)	7	14	0	13	3	0	13	19	0	1	6	1	5
London	8	0	0	11	0	0	14	8	0	1	9	1	11
Stornoway ...	4	15	0	8	2	0	8	11	0	1	0	1	0
Tiree	3	2	0	5	6	0	5	12	0		7		9
Wick	5	1	0	8	13	0	9	3	0	1	0		11
Inverness and													
Benbecula ...	2	18	0	4	19	0	5	5	0		7		9
Kirkwall (Orkney)	3	1	0	5	4	0	5	9	0		7		7
Lerwick (Shetland)	5	13	0	9	13	0	10	5	0	1	2	1	1
London	10	19	0	15	18	0	19	14	0	2	4	2	4
Stornoway ...	2	18	0	4	19	0	5	5	0		7		9
Wick	2	6	0	3	18	0	4	3	0		6		6
Kirkwall (Orkney) and													
Lerwick (Shetland)	2	19	0	5	3	0	5	8	0		7		7
London	13	19	0	21	2	0	25	2	0	2	10	2	10
Lerwick (Shetland) and													
London	15	10	0	23	15	0	27	18	0	3	2	3	2
Stornoway and													
Barra	2	19	0	5	0	0	5	6	0		7		9
London	12	14	0	19	0	0	22	17	0	2	8	2	10
Tiree	3	9	0	5	18	0	6	4	0		8		11
Tiree and													
Barra	1	15	0	2	18	0	3	1	0		4		9
Wick and													
Kirkwall (Orkney)	1	8	0	2	8	0	2	11	0		4		4
Lerwick (Shetland)	3	16	0	6	11	0	6	18	0		9		9
London	12	17	0	19	5	0	23	3	0	2	8	2	8

† Minimum charge is as for 1 Kg. or 1s. 6d., whichever is the greater.
Quantity consignments benefit from percentage rebates by scale. Particulars of such rebates and special commodity rates may be obtained upon application.

BRITISH EUROPEAN AIRWAYS

Member of the International Air Transport Association
Head Office : Northolt, Middlesex

INFORMATION AND BOOKING OFFICES

ABERDEEN
B.E.A. Terminal, Joint Station — Telegram **Bealine, Phone**; Telephone **Aberdeen 8547/9**

BARRA
Angus Macpherson, Post Office, Northbay — Telegram **Bealine, Phone, Castlebay**; Telephone **Northbay 201**

BELFAST
B.E.A., 4, Donegall Square East — Telegram **Bealine, Phone**; Telephone **Belfast 26817**

BENBECULA
B.E.A., Balivanich — Telegram **Bealine, Phone, Nunton**; Telephone **Benbecula 211**

CAMPBELTOWN
James MacGeachy, Union Street — Telephone **Campbeltown 2383**
B.E.A., Machrihanish Airport — Telegram **Bealine, Phone**; Telephone **Machrihanish 240**

EDINBURGH
B.E.A. Terminal, Princes St. Stn. — Telegram **Bealine, Phone**; Telephone **Edinburgh 34823/4**

GLASGOW
B.E.A., Terminal, St. Enoch Station — Telegram **Bealine, Phone, Glasgow**; Telephone **Central 9311/2***
British European Airways, Renfrew Airport — Telegram **Bealine, Phone, Renfrew**; Telephone **Renfrew 2231**
All requests by telephone for reservations to be made to* **Renfrew 2231

INVERNESS
British European Airways, Railway Station, Inverness — Telegram **Bealine, Phone**; Telephone **Inverness 720/1**

ISLAY
B.E.A., Glenegedale Airport — Telegram **Bealine, Phone, Port Ellen**; Telephone **Port Ellen 22**

LONDON
B.E.A. Booking Office, Dorland Hall, Regent Street, S.W. 1 — Telegram **Bealine, Wire**; Telephone **Gerrard 9833**
Passenger Terminal, 194-200 Kensington High Street, W. 8 — Telephone **Western 7227**

ORKNEY
B.E.A., 7, Broad Street, Kirkwall — Telegram **Bealine, Phone, Kirkwall**; Telephone **Kirkwall 159**

SHETLAND
B.E.A., Sumburgh Airport — Telegram **Bealine, Phone, Lerwick**; Telephone **Sumburgh 3**
Ganson Bros., Ltd., Lerwick — Telephone **Lerwick 11**
J. Leask & Sons, Lerwick — Telephone **Lerwick 48**

STORNOWAY
B.E.A., Stornoway Airport — Telegram **Bealine, Phone**; Telephone **Stornoway 256** (after 3 p.m. No. 251)

TIREE
Colin McPhail, Crossapol House — Telegram **Bealine, Phone, Scarinish**; Telephone **Scarinish 9**

WICK
B.E.A., 8, Bridge Street — Telegram **Bealine, Phone**; Telephone **Wick 94**

AND PRINCIPAL TRAVEL AGENCIES

YOU CAN BOOK THROUGH

NO BOOKING FEE

Printed by McCorquodale & Co., Ltd., Glasgow and London, and published by British European Airways Corporation, Head Office, Northolt, Middlesex

7216/28m/12/48(952)

SCOTTISH SERVICES — Sc 9

BEA

TIMETABLE FROM
3 JANUARY 1949
UNTIL FURTHER NOTICE

This timetable is subject to alteration without notice
The timetables of other BEA routes and information on connecting services of BOAC and BSAA may be obtained on request

BEA

BRITISH EUROPEAN AIRWAYS

When BEA absorbed the majority of the Scottish airline activities after the war, there was considerable tension created on many routes where good and reliable, dependable individuals had run schedules with a personal devotion to customers that was completely lacking in the BEA operation. At that time, BEA was operated by people who did not have the understanding of the market and, one has to say, little contemplation of the operating conditions concomitant with running a schedule of any sort under typical Scottish conditions of weather. Many of the older generation of pilots still practised navigation by local knowledge of land, landmark, sea and experience. And BEA initially operated the wrong type of aircraft which, while suited well to English airports and some of the larger Scottish ones, were ill-chosen for the smaller and as-yet unpaved fields. That said, changes were inevitable and this timetable from 1949 illustrates upon its front the new airliner which was joining the Pionair or Dakota in service – the Vickers Viking. Eventually BEAs reorganisation brought a better understanding of the working environment but in the early days it was nothing if not uphill work for airport operators and passengers alike!

Similar names often cause confusion. The pre-war Scottish Airways was formed on August 1st 1937 by the merger of Highland Airways, itself the result of a merger with United Airways and Northern & Scottish Airways, to operate the internal airline interests of British Airways Ltd. It ceased operations at the outset of war in September 1939. In January 1946 a new company was registered called Scottish Airlines to operate a service between Prestwick and Belfast. Later it introduced a service between Reykjavik and Prestwick but only months after it was formed it moved its UK base from Scotland to Croydon. In February 1947, all the internal routes run by small operators such as Scottish Airlines were absorbed into British European Airways. Scottish Airlines, which was associated with Scottish Aviation Ltd, continued flying some routes under its own name, predominantly the Prestwick-Burtonwood-Northolt service using DC-3 aircraft. Here is one of their distinctive bright red luggage labels.

NAME OF PASSENGER
SEAT NO.

CALEDONIAN AIRWAYS
The Scottish International Airline

PASSENGER TICKET AND BAGGAGE CHECK
Your attention is drawn to the Conditions of Contract printed on pages 1-3 of this ticket

A blast from the past! Caledonian Airways (Prestwick) was a wholly private, independent Scottish charter airline founded in April 1961 with one second-hand Douglas DC-7C. The man behind the company was the Scottish entrepreneur Adam Thompson (1926-2000) who was knighted in 1983. He had flown Vickers Viscounts for British European Airways. With business partner John de la Haye, a one-time BEA flight steward who had also managed Cunard Eagle's New York office, and three other colleagues they founded Caledonian Airways with a capital of just £54,000 raised from investors on both sides of the Atlantic. The fledgling company's first flight took place from Gatwick on November 29th, 1961, and the first fare-paying passengers to New York left Prestwick on December 21st, 1961. The return fare was £40. The business expanded rapidly over the following years to the point where, by the end of the 1960s, it had become the leading Transatlantic 'affinity group' charter operator. It saw passenger numbers rise from 8,000 in 1961 to 800,000 in 1970, this representing 22.7% of all British non-scheduled airline passengers. Along with this it was the nation's most consistently profitable and financially most secure independent airline and throughout its ten years of existence it never failed to make a profit. By the end of 1970, the airline operated eleven aircraft, all jets, and engaged primarily on group charters between North America, Europe and the Far East using Boeing 707s, as well as general charter and inclusive tour activities in Europe utilising One-Elevens. The airline took pains to emphasise its origins and on each side of the fuselage of its aircraft as well as the name 'Caledonian' was the phrase 'The Scottish International Airline'. Additionally, its stewardesses wore tartan uniforms. The in-flight service for passengers was deliberately good even though the prices were cheaper than those of scheduled airlines and the airline rapidly earned a reputation for the quality of its service and in-flight meals. In its 1963-64 financial year, the airline carried 110,700 passengers and made a net profit of £90,600. By 1970, Caledonian was carrying the majority of the approximately 1.4 million passengers flying across the Atlantic each year as members of affinity groups. The long-term goal of its founders was to run a fully-fledged scheduled operation. They considered Caledonian's transformation into a scheduled operator the only way to build an airline with a long-term, stable future. However, applications for a licence to operate Transatlantic scheduled services were rejected by the ATLB while allowing it other scheduled routes including, in 1966, Scotland to the Mediterranean destinations. As other organisations clamoured to buy into Caledonian Airlines the outcome was some subtle changes in the pattern of the airline. Fresh applications for licences were the subject of objections by other operators including BOAC. Matters came to a head late in November 1970 when, with fresh injections of capital from major investors, Caledonian acquired British United Airways (BUA) together with its fleet of aircraft. BUA had been formed in the summer of 1960 by the re-naming of Airwork Ltd. At that time, BUA was the largest contemporary independent airline and leading private sector scheduled carrier in the United Kingdom. For a while the merged business operated as Caledonian//BUA before adopting the name British Caledonian in September 1971. For the next twenty years, 'B-CAL' as it was dubbed was without doubt Britain's largest independent, international scheduled airline, having a global route network serving more than 40 destinations in some 25 countries on five continents.

For a long time, Adam Thompson's Scottish international airline, Caledonian Airways, was not taken seriously by other operators in the market. He started operating in April, 1961, with one leased DC-7C but, finding and exploiting his niche market – namely the so-called 'affinity' groups' charter work – his business expanded rapidly. By the dawn of 1970 Caledonian Airways was operating an all-jet fleet of eleven aircraft. In November that year it merged with British United Airways to form British Caledonian Airways – the largest 'second force' airline in Britain. Here is one of the airline's picture postcards given out to passengers so that they could spread the message. It depicts the company's Bristol B.175 Britannia 312, G-AOVI, which was acquired second hand in or about 1965. The aircraft was withdrawn from use at Luton on January 16th, 1972, and, having languished in the open for five years, was broken up in April 1977.

Scottish European Airways was another short-lived post-war endeavour. Set up on April 27th, 1988, it was based in Paisley and had one leased aircraft – HS-748 G-BPFU. It offered services to Brussels, Frankfurt, Newcastle, Edinburgh and Glasgow but seems to have quietly faded from the scene in mid-1990 leaving nothing behind but a small pocket timetableÉ

BOOKING OFFICES

United Kingdom
Scottish European Airways Ltd
Glasgow Airport, Paisley
Scotland PA3 2SG
Reservations: Tel: 041-887 2244
Administration: Tel: 041-887 7700
Telex: 776878 Fax: 041-887 0867

Belgium
Scottish European Airways
VilvoorDelaan 153 B
B 1930 Zaventem Belgium
Reservations: (02) 725 3435
Flight Information: (02) 723 03 11

West Germany
Scottish European Airways
Brentano Straße 17
6000 Frankfurt/Main
Reservations: (069) 72 06 49
Flight Information: (069) 239430/230956

Your travel agent

Scottish European
AIRWAYS

Timetable
Effective 30th July '89

At the end of the Second World War, Glasgow's original Moorpark Aerodrome, long known as Renfrew Airport, underwent an extensive modernisation and improvement. Its redesign was placed in the hands of the Forfar-born architect, Sir William Hardie Kininmonth (1904-88). Kininmonth had studied under Sir Edward Lutyens and worked with Sir Basil Spence. Not surprisingly, his design for Renfrew's facilities was dramatic and revealed the influences of both the Art Deco movement and Le Corbusier. Its stunning interiors were light and airy while his great arched fa◉ade was a clear statement for Glasgow. The new airport entrance and terminal was formally opened in 1954 but would exist for a mere dozen years before the recognition that it was too small. In May of 1966 the airport was closed, activities being transferred to the larger (and close-by) Abbotsinch. This picture postcard view depicts the entrance to Renfrew shortly after its expensive re-vamp: it was later razed to the ground and today nothing survives. *Picture from the collection of Richard Stenlake.*

On May 2nd, 1966, Vickers 802 Viscount, G-AOHV, became the first commercial service to land at the newly-opened Abbotsinch Airport. This marked the effective closure of Glasgow's original but now too small Renfrew Airport to commercial flights. The opening flight arrived from Edinburgh piloted by Captain Eric Starling who was BEA's Scottish flight manager. During its first year of operation, the airport handled 1.5m passengers and 34,000 aircraft movements. Renfrew would soon disappear under the inevitable tide of housing and industrial development.

A bleak day at Glasgow's new Abbotsinch Airport in the 1960s. Vickers Viscount 302 G-AOHS is parked at a gate with BAC One-Eleven G-ASJC behind. A second BAC taxies away to the right as another Viscount takes to the air in the background.

When Vickers Aircraft Ltd attempted to capitalise on the enormous world wide success of its Viscount turboprop airliner, it made the grave mistake of making another turboprop machine instead of a pure jet. The Vanguard was a good aircraft but it was obsolescent before it was launched. It was the maker's third different type of aircraft to bear that name only it wasn't to be a case of 'third time lucky'. BEA ordered at least 20 of the 139-seaters of which this one, G-APEB, was the second, first flown in July 1979. Here it is seen on a wet day at Abbotsinch being serviced for flight. This aircraft was withdrawn from use at Heathrow on March 31st, 1973, and subsequently broken up. Most were converted to freighter configuration with an enormous side door on the port side.

A wet day at Abbotsinch as two Viscounts are prepared on the apron. Nearest the camera is G-AOJE, a model 802 first registered on March 6th, 1956 and bearing the joint logos of Scottish Airways and BEA. This aircraft enjoyed a long service life before being broken up at Cardiff in August 1981. The second aircraft visible to the right is a model 802C, G-AOHM, first registered on January 2nd, 1956 and bearing the markings of Channel Islands Airways – one of the regular 'long-distance' internal services in the British Isles. This aircraft was sold to Kenya on May 21st 1999 ultimately becoming 3D-OHM.

BAC One-Eleven Series 501 G-AWYU of British Caledonian pictured in 1969. A popular aircraft in its time it was liked by pilots and passengers alike.

One of the promotional postcards published by British Caledonian Airways illustrating its McDonnell Douglas DC10-30. Curiously, on this picture the registration letters have been air-brushed out.

Most pre-war aerodromes were developed around simple features, a good pasture and associated buildings. Prestwick Airport was no exception. Close to the original field was one of Scotland's minor stately homes – Orangefield House – and this would gradually be transformed into the passenger terminal. And when there was a need for a proper control tower for air traffic control, the original four chimneys of the house were filled with concrete to create piles to support a great superstructure on top. And in the way of things all this was ultimately swept away in the advance of purpose-built structures. This shows what the terminal building and control tower looked like in the 1930s. *Picture from the collection of Richard Stenlake.*

Prestwick was always a delightfully rural airport, in some way reminiscent of the very first Croydon airport before it was developed across Plough Lane. This is the entrance as it was back in the early 1930s. *Picture from the collection of Richard Stenlake.*

As an international terminal airport, Prestwick was ideally situated in flat terrain which enjoyed ideal visibility and freedom from bad weather for most of the year. The view from the control tower was suitably Arcadian. The majority of aircraft are American military, there being three Douglas DC-3 and one DC-4 in US markings. Of interest is the only civil machine in sight – the Trans Canada Air Lines' C-54GM, CF-TEM. Essentially a Rolls-Royce Merlin-powered unpressurised Douglas C-64G, the type was known in the RCAL as the North Star M1, also described as the DC-4M. This particular aircraft was built to TCA specification and leased to them on January 21st, 1947, being returned to the RCAF on March 4th, 1949. Based with No.412 Sqdn, RCAF, at Uplands, Ontario, it was maintained as a North Star Mk.M1-ST for VIP passenger transport and carried members of the British royal family as well as the Canadian prime minister on many occasions. CF-TEM met its end in a take-off crash at Hall Beach Airport, Northern Territories. As for Trans Canada Air Lines, set up in 1937 as the nation's national carrier, the name was changed in 1965 to Air Canada. *Picture from the collection of Richard Stenlake.*

With its extended runways, Prestwick became an ideal transatlantic jumping-off point to join and later replace Ireland's Shannon Airport. Many European airlines refuelled here en route for the 'crossing of the puddle'. Here a BOAC Bristol Britannia disgorges passengers the old way – via wheeled steps and the open atmosphere. *Picture from the collection of Richard Stenlake.*

Much of the development of aviation in Scotland is down to the efforts of one man, David Fowler McIntyre. Born at Ibrox, Govan, in 1905 he came to the attention of the aviation world in 1933 when he was pilot to the Houston Mount Everest Flight Expedition. Joining No.602 *City of Glasgow Squadron* he eventually became its commanding officer and attained the rank of wing commander. He established Prestwick Airport and formed Scottish Aviation Ltd which, during the war, carried out numerous aircraft conversions and repairs. In post-war years, his company made a business of converting surplus Douglas DC-3 Dakota aircraft (among others) into airliners with properly-upholstered interiors. His company designed and produced several ground-breaking STOL aircraft including the Pioneer and Twin Pioneer. It was in one of the latter that, hastening to a potential customer to give a demonstration, he and two others were to lose their lives when the aircraft broke up in mid-air. The accident took place on December 8th, 1957, in the Libyan desert near Tripoli. This picture, taken in McIntyre's office during April 1953, shows him with a terrestrial globe and hints at his aspirations for a worldwide airline operation. *Picture courtesy Dougal McIntyre.*

Scotland's Loganair airline began in 1962 as the air taxi arm of a construction company but within two years had embarked on operating a scheduled service to the Outer Hebrides. Britten-Norman's BN-2 Islander was consciously designed as a Rapide replacement offering more engine power, 'char-a-banc'-style seating (continuous rows with no central aisle). The first production aircraft was G-ATWU, first flown at the Bembridge, Isle of Wight, factory on August 20th, 1966, was painted up with the Loganair name and loaned for evaluation flights as seen here. This particular airframe was used to develop the stretched BN-2E and, later, to the prototype Trislander.

Britten-Norman Islander G-BPCA works a typical service from a beach. Seen here accelerating for take-off, the moist air has created a curious series of vortices from the propeller tips giving the impression of four engines.

The Britten-Norman Trislander was a triple-engined variant of the twin-engined Islander. G-BDOS was delivered to Loganair in November 1976 and served until April 1982 when it was sold on. The aircraft was particular popular because of its semi-STOL performance which made many of the Island airports and landing strips accessible to this 18-seater.

Flying in the colours of British Airways, a DHC.6-310 Twin Otter, G-BVVK, lands on the sands at Barra demonstrating one of the oldest forms of aerodrome runway but one for which flight schedules always carried the caveat 'subject to tides'. This Loganair route was also flown by Britten-Norman Islander aircraft. The Twin Otter seen here was formerly LN-BEZ and joined the fleet on December 21st, 1994.

Loganair franchise FlyBe taking off from Abbotsinch. The aircraft is a SAAB-Scania 340B, G-LGNA which was registered to the company on June 11th, 1999.

The Short SC-7 Skyvan was a low-cost airliner derived from work carried out by F G Miles Ltd and employing the Hurel Dubois high aspect-ratio wing. Shorts of Belfast acquired the design project and all rights to the Miles' design known as the HGM.106 Caravan. However, Shorts realised that the extremely long span concomitant with the French-designed wing would make it unsuitable for the very purposes proposed for it – short-range high-capacity work from unprepared airfields and small maintenance hangars. Shorts designed a wholly-new project around a utility fuselage and having a strut-braced 64-feet span wing which would carry 3,000 lbs of freight or fifteen passengers using a pair of supercharged Continental piston engines. Soon these would be replaced by French TurbomŽca Astazou turbofans and, later still, Garrett-AiResearch engines. Here G-AWYG is seen in Loganair colours. First flown on January 25th, 1969, it was based at Abbotsinch.

FlyBe is one of those modern businesses hampered by a name that seems to have been generated by a computer fault. It was originally called Jersey European Airways but changed its name to British European but then took over BA Connect in 2007 to create the FlyBe Group. On January 17th, 2008, in what the company called 'a historic deal' it signed a franchise deal with Loganair to operate services in Scotland and also some in Ireland. Here Highland Airways' Scottish Aviation Jetstream G-BTXG poses next to a De Havilland Canada DHC-6-300 Twin Otter of FlyBe at Benbecula.

Loganair built up a 14-strong fleet of SAAB 340 aircraft the first of which, a model 340-AF registered G-GNTB, is pictured here at delivery in December 2003. Equipped as a 33-34-seater, these Swedish twin turbo-powered aircraft were already considered obsolescent: the product of a joint deal between the American Fairchild company before it pulled out of aviation in 1985, and the Swedish SAAB company, the design first flew in January 1983. Some 459 were built at Linkšping before production ceased in 1999. Six years later, SAAB withdrew completely from civil aviation production. This picture shows the all-white aircraft on the apron at Benbecula.

Turnhouse was first opened in 1915 by the Royal Flying Corps. Gradually the grass field was expanded and hard runways laid down. Its strategic position – seven miles west of Edinburgh and 46 miles east of Glasgow – combined with its flat terrain suggested early on that it would make a good civilian aerodrome but it wasn't until the RAF finally departed in 1997 that the field was developed as Edinburgh Airport. Here, in gentler times, Chipmunks of No.12 AEF are seen awaiting refuelling after a day's flying. In the background is a Scottish Aviation Bulldog. It is April 9th, 1992.

Chipmunks of No.12 AEF (Air Experience Flight) at Turnhouse. Pictured on September 8th 1967, WP970, a T.10, sits with two others outside the maintenance hangar. *Picture by Ruth A Scholefield.*

Refuelling the Chipmunk T.10 two-seaters at Turnhouse using the 'snorkel-bowser' on the evening of April 9th, 1992. In the background, WB587 is just airborne on the last flight of the day.

The sea has always been our oldest ally and enemy, depending what you are using it for. Lighthouses once formed an aid to shipping that was absolutely indispensable. Aviation came to improve the lives of the lighthouse keepers whose reliance on boats for supplies was oft disrupted by weather and the sea itself. From the 1960s onwards, helicopters were increasingly used to service our many coastal lights and Oban was the depot for the Edinburgh-based Northern Lighthouse Board. From Oban supplies were flown to many a light including Smeaton's Eilean Musdile in Oban itself and overlooking the Sound of Kerrera. Pictured on September 19th, 1974, we see parked on the pad at the NLB'd Oban depot an MBB Bo.105, G-AZOR, on charter from Management Aviation, today's Bond Offshore Hellicopter. As with virtually every other light around the British Isles, Scotland's lighthouses are today either superseded thanks to satellite navigation or are fully automated. The lonely life of the lighthouse keeper has, as a profession vanished. *Picture from the collection of Richard Stenlake.*

RAF Station Leuchars lies right on the coast and when there were high tides and storm surges, the sea invaded the extreme east of the airfield. In one of the quirks of modern planning, the area most prone to flooding back in the 1940s is now partly given over to housing. The sea defences must have improved since my day! In 1950 this was the home of No.43 Squadron which had re-equipped with Gloster Meteor F.8 twin-jet fighters. This is WA849 parked in the autumn sun displaying its squadron black and white chequerboard markings.

Viewed from the front against a backdrop of wooden radio masts, Meteor WA849 awaits its next call into the blue. A mishap to one of the Squadron aircraft involved another Meteor. Its pilot cocked up his approach and overshot on landing, touching down too far along the runway. Instead of going round again, he decided to make it stick and so 'stood on the brakes'. Just off the end of the runway was a squat, square concrete blockhouse. As the end of the runway raced up, the chap in the cockpit put on hard rudder and yanked even harder on the brakes (really it was merely a little squeeze lever on the control column). The Meteor swung through ninety degrees and, still travelling at a really impressive rate, struck the blockhouse with a sickening thud. The nose just missed, but the full force of the square-on impact was taken by the port engine nacelle. This actually concertina'd into a series of concentric rings rather like the bellows of an old camera. It was most impressive, especially as the nacelle was now quite flush with the leading edge of the wing. The pilot was by this time a strange hue of white and blue and was not seen around too much after that. The impact also twisted the fuselage, the tailplane ending up at an unfamiliar angle to the rest of the aircraft. The concrete blockhouse was quite undamaged save for some silver paint scrapes.

Hawker Hunter F.4 WV318 at Lossiemouth, Moray. Part of the defence structure operating during the Cold War, No.8 Squadron was one of those ready to counter any incursions into British airspace by Soviet aircraft.

By 1960 Britain's politicians had hobbled the aircraft industry so we suddenly had a shortage of home-defence aircraft. We had scrapped our own brilliant next-generation fighters, the TSR.2 and the Hawker Siddeley P.1154, for a short-term economic gain. Now we had to 'buy foreign' to equip our armed forces. The McDonnell Douglas Phantom twin-jet long-range supersonic fighter, already in use by our Navy, was chosen. Described as a 'large' machine, it has a top speed in excess of Mach 2.2 and could tote a load of more than 18,000 lbs (that's over eight tons) of weaponry on nine external hardpoints. A noisy aircraft as will be confirmed by those walkers in the Highlands exposed to the low-level training antics of the thing, the FGR.2 seen here in September 1970 has been used by a number of squadrons including both 43 and 111 based at Leuchars.

An interesting legacy of the 'Cold War' years remembered in this picture of No.11 Squadron's gang at Leuchars in June, 1967. Having been stood down several years earlier, 11 Squadron re-formed in Fife on 1st April of that year with some brand-new Lightning F.6 jets in order to fill a gap in the UK air defences. Leuchars was a key station with the job of patrolling the most northerly UK air defence zone. This extended well out past the Danish Faroe Islands towards Iceland and including the Faroes Gap, a most inhospitable environment and not a place in which to miss a join-up with the flight-refuelling tanker or suffer any serious failure of the aircraft. It was this area which received most intrusions from long-range Soviet reconnaissance aircraft, and the Leuchars QRA (Quick Reaction Alert) had numerous encounters with marauding Bears, Bisons and Badgers. In June 1967 the squadron assembled for this group photograph:

Left to right, rear: 'Lofty' Lance, Harry Drew, Rich Rhodes, Peter Colling, David Blacke
Wally Hill, Mike Laughlan, Dave Eggleton, Bob Priest.
Front, left to right: Keven Mace, John Anders, John Fawcett, Dave Trick, Geoff Fish, Brian Clifford, Brian Fuller.

The English Electric Lightning F.2 was a supersonic front-line defence aircraft which played a vital part during the Cold War era. The first (and only) all-British Mach 2 fighter and provided with what were, for its time, advanced avionics, the Lightning was renowned for its ability as an interceptor. The type first flew in 1954 and by the time it retired from active service in 1988, 337 had been built. Performing a major role in Britain's strategic air defence several squadrons, including numbers 19 and 92, were stationed in Scotland, notably Lossiemouth and Leuchars. Here we see an example taking part as a static exhibited at an RAF 'open day'. After English Electric was integrated into the British Aircraft Corporation conglomerate, the type became known as the BAC Lightning.

Pre-flighting aeroplanes in olden times involved petrol, oil and a few bullets, perhaps, even, a bomb or two and not forgetting the 'trolleyacc' external battery for the starter motor. Today's aircraft demonstrate advanced hypochondria and need pacifying with all manner of odd aids. Here an English Electric Lightning F.6 XS936 of No.23 Squadron stands on dispersal at RAF Leuchars in 1965. It is surrounded by cylinders of nitrogen needed to inert the fuel tanks to prevent them from exploding as fuel is burned off. Observe the nifty 'loft-ladder' needed to enable the pilot to ascend to his neatly-lidded command-post in the front end. Somebody observing the nose of this aircraft was heard to comment that it must be for particularly large lemonsÉ

SEPECAT Jaguar GR.1 of No.6 Squadron pictured at Lossiemouth in the late 1970s. Since 1936, the structure of the Royal Air Force had been built around three operational groups named Fighter Command, Bomber Command and Coastal Command. Now with the post-war retrenchment in full swing yet with the Cold War threats as real as ever, it was decided that it would be more efficient to amalgamate the groups under one umbrella organisation to be called RAF Strike Command. In 1968, the new Command was created with the former Fighter and Bomber wings, Coastal Command joining in November 1969.

The Hawker Siddeley Nimrod MR.1 and MR.2 have enjoyed a long and happy association with Scotland stretching back some four decades. As the RAF's key maritime patrol and surveillance aircraft throughout the Cold War, this de Havilland Comet airliner derivative saw service with a number of squadrons, predominantly 120, 291, 206 and 42 at Kinloss. This picture shows XV241 in its MR.1 form before modification, which including the fitting of an in-flight refuelling probe above the nose. The type was withdrawn from use a year earlier than projected, XV241 being decommissioned at Kinloss on March 1st, 2010. Despite a nationwide outcry at the scrapping of these useful aircraft which still had several years of good service left in them, they were cut up for scrap. XV241's nose was, however, preserved and is today in the National Museum of Flight at East Fortune, East Lothian.

The Hawker Siddeley HS.801 Nimrod was a maritime patrol and surveillance aircraft widely employed at Scottish bases during the Cold War. XV230, a Nimrod MR.2P, was photographed at Lossiemouth in 1985 where it was operated by 120 Squadron having replaced the Shackletons both it and No.8 Squadron formally operated.

It was not only British aircraft that used Scotland's facilities. Here is a USAF F-16A Fighting Falcon assigned to 388th Tactical Fighter Wing (TFW) pictured undergoing routine servicing at Lossiemouth in June 1981 when it took part in the Strike Command Tactical Bombing exercise held jointly by the Royal Air Force and the United States Air Force. For this exercise, the aircraft bore the number 4 represented in white on the fin and in large black format on the rudder. This aircraft subsequently returned to the States where it crashed into Great Salt Lake, Utah, killing the pilot on January 19th, 1983. *Picture by Don Sutherland.*

To end on a quiet note after all those jets, here's the silent world of gliding. Where once high-performance sailplanes came out of Yorkshire's Kirkybymoorside and the little woodwork factory of Fred Slingsby, today's top gliders come from Europe. This Schempp-Hirth Discus, G-JPIP, was built by Orlican in the Czech Republic. With its elegant 20-metre span this aircraft takes full advantage of the fantastic conditions that Scotland can offer in the way of soaring. The machine is seen here operated by the Scottish Gliding Centre at Portmoak Airfield. *Picture with grateful acknowledgement to Ronald Richardson.*

Bibliography

[Anon]: From Blackburn to BAE Systems: Robert Blackburn and his Legacy 1909-2005. BAE Systems, 2006.

Archer, Ed: *Flying at Lanark.* Stenlake Publishing, Catrine, 2010

Bao, Phil Lo: *An Illustrated History of British European Airways.* Brocombe, Middlesex, 1989

- , and Hutchison, Iain: *BEAline to the Islands.* Kea Publishing, Erskine, Renfrew, 2002

Berry, Peter: *Prestwick Airport & Scottish Aviation*, Tempus, Gloucestershire, 2005

Bridgeman, Leonard [and others]: *Jane's All The World's Aircraft.* Samson Low, London, var editions, 1945-1971

British Aircraft Industry 1948, *The;* [Directory] SBAC, London, 1948.

Calderwood, Roy: *Times Subject to Tides: the Story of Barra Airport.* Kea, Renfrew, 1999

Cameron, Dugald: *Glasgow's Airport.* Holmes McDougall, Edinburgh, 1990

Clegg, Peter V: *Flying Against the Elements.* Aberdeen Museum & Art Gallery, 1987

- : *Sword in the Sky.* GMS Enterprises, Peterborough, 1990

- : *Wings over the Glens.* GMS Enterprises, Peterborough, 1995

Cobham, Sir Alan John: *A Time to Fly.* Shepheard-Walwyn, London, 1978

Cook, John: *Air Transport: The First Fifty Years.* Archive Photographs Series, Stroud, 1997.

Doyle, Neville: *The Triple Alliance: the predecessors of the first British Airways.* Air-Britain, Tonbridge, 2001.

Easson, Ian: *The Scottish Gliding Union: A History 1934-2008.* IKE Publishing, Creiff, 2008.

Ferguson, James D: *The Story of Aberdeen Airport.* Scottish Airports, Glasgow, 1984

Fergusson, Sir James [of Kilkerran]: *Balloon Tytler.* Faber & Faber, London, 1972

Fresson, E E: *Air Road to the Isles: Memoirs of Capt E E Fresson.* David Rendel, London, 1967

Galbraith, Ann: *The Dream that would not Die: The 50-year Fight for Prestwick Airport.* Exit Zero, New Jersey, 2009

Gillies, J Douglas, and Wood, J L: *Aviation in Scotland.* Royal Aeronautical Society, Glasgow, 1966.

Grey, Charles Grey: *Jane's All the World's Aircraft.* Sampson Low Marston, London, var.eds 1945-1980.

Halford-MacLeod, Guy: *Britain's Airlines, Vol 1; 1946-1951.* Tempus, Gloucestershire, 2006 (rep. 2011)

- : *Britain's Airlines, Vol 2; 1951-1964.* Tempus, Gloucestershire, 2007

- : *Britain's Airlines, Vol 3; 1964 to Deregulation.* History Press, Gloucestershire, 2010

Higham, Robin: *The British Rigid Airship, 1908-1931.* Foulis, London, 1961

Hobson, Chris: *Scottish Aviation Pioneer CC.Mk.1.* Aviation News. Alan W Hall (Pubs), Edgware, n.d. [1980]

Hutchison, Iain: *The Story of Loganair.* Western Isles Publishing, Stornoway, 1987

- : *The Flight of the Starling.* Kea Publishing, Erskine, Renfrew, 1992

- : *Air Ambulance: Sixty Years of the Scottish Air Ambulance Service.* Kea Publishing, Erskine, Renfrew, 2005

Jackson, Aubrey Joseph: *British Civil Aircraft 1919-1959.* [2 vols] Putnam, London, 1959.

- : *British Civil Aircraft 1919-1972.* [3 vols] Putnam, London, 1973.

Jarrett, Philip: *Another Icarus: Story of Percy Pilcher.* Smithsonian Institution, Washington, USA, 1987

Jones, A C Merton: *British Independent Airlines 1946-1976* [4 vols]. LAAS International, Uxbridge, 1976. 2.ed [one vol]. Aviation Hobby Shop, West Drayton, 2000

Kay, Charles E Mac: *Beardmore Aviation 1913-1930.* MacKay, Glasgow, 2012.

Lake, Deborah: *Tartan Air Force: Scotland and a century of Military Aviation.* Birlinn, Edinburgh, 2007.

McCloskey, Keith: *Edinburgh Airport, A History.* History Press, Stroud, 2013.

- : *Glasgow's Airports: Renfrew & Abbotsinch.* History Press, Stroud, 2009.

McIntyre, Dougal: *Prestwick's Pioneer: a Portrait of David F McIntyre.* Woodfield Publishing, Bognor Regis, 2004

May, Gary: *The Challenge of BEA.* Wolfe, London, 1971

Middleton, Edgar: *The Great War in the Air. [4 vols.]* Waverley, London, 1920

Oakley, Charles Allen: *Aircraft Construction in Scotland: The Future of the Flying Boat.* Institute of Engineers & Shipbuilders in Scotland, Glasgow, 1946

Ord-Hume, Arthur W J G: *British Light Aeroplanes: Their Evolution, Development & Perfection 1920-1940.* GMS Enterprises, Peterborough, 2000.

- : *British Commercial Aircraft: Their Evolution, Development & Perfection 1920-1940.* GMS Enterprises, Peterborough, 2003.

- : *British Private Aircraft 1946-1970.* Vols. 1 & 2, MMP, Petersfield, 2011, 2013.

- : *Autogiro: Rotary Wings before the Helicopter.* MMP, Petersfield, 2009.

- : *The Lympne Trials: Searching for an Ideal Light Plane.* Stenlake, Catrine, 2012

Penrose, Harald James: *British Aviation: The Pioneer Years.* Putnam, London, 1967.

Reed, Arthur: *Britain's Aircraft Industry – What West Right? What Went Wrong?* Dent, London, 1973.

Robertson, Alan: *Lion Rampant and Winged: A Commemorative History of Scottish Aviation Ltd.* Robertson, Barassie, 1986

Sherry, Alan M: *The Blackburn: Dumbarton's Aircraft Factory.* Stenlake, Catrine, 1996; rep. 2008

Smith, David J: *Action Stations 7; Military Airfields of Scotland...&c.* Patrick Stephens, Cambridge, 1983

Smith, Harry: *One Foot on the Ground.* Cirrus Associates, Dorset, 2002.

Smith, Ronald: *British Built Aircraft.* Vol. 5. Tempus, Stroud, 2005.

Staddon, Thomas G: *A History of Cambrian Airways.* Airline Publications, Hounslow, 1979.

Stroud, John: *Railway Air Services.* Ian Allan, Shepperton, 1987

Walker, Percy Brooksbank: *Early Aviation at Farnborough.* Vol.2 *The First Aeroplanes.* Macdonald, London, 1974

Warner, Guy: *Orkney by Air: A Photographic Journey Through Time.* Kea Publishing, Renfrew, 2005

Webster, Jack: *The Flying Scots: A Century of Aviation in Scotland.* Glasgow Royal Concert Hall, Glasgow, 1994

Wiggins, Paul R, and Reid, Alan J: *Scotland Scanned.* Central Scotland Aviation Group, Glasgow, 1973

INDEX

IFC = inside front cover; IBC inside back cover; OBC outside back cover; numbers in **bold** type signify illustrations.